HENTZ *Of Things Not Seen*

HENTZ *Of Things Not Seen*

BY HARRIET HENTZ HOUSER

The Macmillan Company

New York   1955

To Anne Frierson Griffin

"Now faith is the substance of things hoped for, the evidence of things not seen."—Hebrews 11:1

FOREWORD

You've probably never read a story exactly like this one. You see, I don't know the ending. Perhaps before I finish telling the story I shall know how it ends. Perhaps I shan't live to know; but somehow I have faith to believe that the ending will be a happy one.

Believing that, enables me to begin this story. After I had made several starts, timidity and fear of criticism overtook me, and I destroyed the manuscript. A year and a half has passed since the first beginning, and the passage of time has made the compulsion to write the story even stronger. I don't think I shall ever be able to sleep well again until I have completed it.

In May, 1951, my son was critically injured. My son is a quadriplegic—meaning that his four extremities are paralyzed. He was a strong, healthy, active boy until that May morning when, at the age of seventeen, he dived from a springboard into water too shallow and hit his head on the bottom of the lake. The blow dislocated his neck between the fourth and fifth cervical vertebrae and also caused injury to his spinal cord. Few people have ever recovered from a similar injury. I know personally two young men who were restored to activity. The mother of one of those boys has been an inspiration to us, and I firmly believe that her faith was responsible for her son's dramatic recovery. The doctors told her from the beginning that her son would not live, but that if he did he would be bedridden. She refused to accept this prognosis, and told the surgeons and the doctors that her son would live and that he would walk again. Even while he wasted away from one hundred and sixty pounds to eighty pounds, she insisted that he would be well. The doctors looked at her with indulgence and pity because of her simple trust. She hadn't seen the things they had seen. However, it was things not seen that gave her faith. Her boy is well. He is Charles L. Van Diviere, Jr., of Brunswick, Georgia. His recovery was reported in the following national magazines: *Newsweek,* June 2nd, 1952; *Forbes,* September 1, 1952; *Science News-Letter,* May 31, 1952.

I dare to believe that my son will get well, even though I kept silent when the doctors said there was no chance for him to live. I lacked the courage to voice my faith. I was not silent because I was ashamed of having faith; but I did shrink from the pity of people who from necessity must be practical-minded.

The earliest writing of this book was a carefully guarded secret. It was something that I could not discuss with my husband or my friends. It could bring embarrassment to our family. Nevertheless, I choose to believe that it can help others to fight on in the face of almost insurmountable obstacles.

I am neither a mystic nor a religious fanatic. I was brought up in a Christian home, for which I am thankful. As I matured I also matured spiritually; but I had no occasion, until the tragedy in our family, to know the depth of that growth, nor to suspect the proportions it would assume. Without the constant consciousness of God's nearness during these past few years, I probably would have lost my mind. This story is a record of the events of those years, of a young boy's courage and faith, and of the love and help of his friends.

I believe that my son lived following his injury for some very good reason. In fact, I have always believed that there was an unusual reason for his being at all. That Nature should have selected me—a creature disinterested in the prospect of caring for a child—to bear a son caused me to think. Neither my husband nor I wanted children. Our attitude was probably a result of the depression years. Children did not fit into the carefree life we had patterned for ourselves.

In 1933 we were living in my husband's home town, Perry, Georgia, which then had a population of about fifteen hundred. Life was simpler then, and we had fun doing things that young married people today would consider quaint. Perhaps our kind of pleasure was enforced by economic necessity, but it was genuine. We had a ladies' baseball team, and I was the heavy hitter! When we first started, the Methodists played the Baptists; but we branched out and scheduled games with ladies' teams from neighboring towns. On the day of one of the big games, I discovered that I was going to have a child. On the way to the game I tripped and fell down a flight of stairs. Despite my fall I played the game, hit a home run and ran round the bases. I remember telling my unborn child— who even then, within such a short time, had assumed a personality for me—that he was hardy and possessed a determined character. I formed a respect for him on that day that I still have. I *knew* it was to be a boy; and I decided then and there that my child's hand lay in that of Destiny.

When my son was seventeen months old I took him to see

a very dear and wise friend who was over seventy-five years old. She had a Doctor of Philosophy degree and was the wife of a minister. Looking at the bright-faced child with the shining eyes and hair, she said something that I have never forgotten, and that expresses quite well what I feel now. As she softly laid her wrinkled hand on his head, she said in whispered reverence, "God surely had something very special in mind when He made this child."

This story was first begun in February, 1952, in New York. Somehow I couldn't go on with it. I have made subsequent starts and put them aside. Doubts assailed my mind, but each time a new surge of interest gripped me. At times the continued seriousness of my son's condition would chill me and shake my faith to such a point that it would seem ridiculous even to me to put words of faith on paper. Those periods were brief. I've been frightened many times when his life seemed such a feeble thing, but only for the briefest moments have I bordered on desperation.

One night recently I couldn't sleep. My son was in the hospital in Macon, Georgia, following his twelfth operation. His condition was critical. Though I knew he would get well, my heart bore a heavy burden. It was then that I picked up the book *A Man Called Peter*, by Catherine Marshall. The chapter "God Still Answers Prayer" convinced me that I must go on with this story. She'd asked God what He wanted *her* to do in order that she might be made well. She said Jesus had always told sick people to *do* something before He healed them. He told her the thing she had to do. I felt a conviction to write about my son, a conviction so real that I could not disregard it. I knew that God would strengthen and guide me in the task, and that somehow others would be helped by the telling of this simple story. God knew that if the faith with which I entered into this period of suffering would grow every day and sustain me, and keep me in joyful hope, then I should tell others about the things that made it grow.

HENTZ *Of Things Not Seen*

CHAPTER ONE

On the morning of May 19, 1951, our telephone rang. It was my husband's sister, Louise, and I heard her sobbing before she spoke. Something dreadful had happened. She barely managed to tell me to go to the little hospital in our town. "Hentz has had an accident."

I jumped into the car and rushed downtown to the hospital, which is just four blocks from our home. A large crowd had gathered outside, as is the custom in a small town when anything unusual takes place. They stared at me, and I tried to read some answer in their faces. As I ran inside, the hospital seemed unusually dark after the brightness of the May sunshine. I hurried down the short hall looking into each of the rooms in an effort to find him. Then I saw him. I saw his blond hair first. He lay on a shiny examination table, still clad in the green nylon swimming trunks of which he was so proud. On one leg of the trunks I had sewed the colorful emblem he'd earned from the National Aquatic School the summer before. I felt a little relief when I saw his beautiful suntanned body whole and unspotted by blood. Not knowing what to expect, I must have been quite pale as I spoke to him because he said, "Don't be afraid, Mother; I'll be all right." Though he didn't sound as though he really thought so, I know now that he did.

My husband, Fred, was standing beside the table on one side, and the doctor was on the other. Though the doctor didn't seem to be alarmed I could see that Fred was. I hoped that it was caused by the shock of hearing that his son had had an accident, and by those first horrible moments of uncertainty. He was so pale! He bit his lip to still the quivering, as if he were keeping something from me. They told me the doctor had made some X-rays. When I asked him if Hentz would be all right, he said, "He'll be all right, but I want to send him to Macon for additional X-rays and for an orthopedic surgeon to examine him."

I went home again to get dressed. When I returned they were taking Hentz to a shining Cadillac ambulance on a stretcher. The crowd was much larger, and the people looked from Hentz to Fred and me. Fred and I got in the back with Hentz. A friend sat with the driver. My husband's chair was near Hentz's bed, and Fred kept saying tender things to him. Hentz was so still. He looked well and talked rationally. I still had no idea as to the exact nature of the injury.

Hentz asked his father, "I won't stay paralyzed, will I, Daddy?" Again and again he asked, "Daddy, will I always be paralyzed?" Fred moved his head out of Hentz's line of vision. Tears were streaming down his face. Only then did I learn that my son was paralyzed. I'd never known anyone who'd fractured a neck or back, and I knew nothing about spinal cords and nerves and muscles.

After we reached the hospital, Hentz was hurried to the X-ray room. He laughed and joked with the young women in attendance; but even though they smiled I sensed their tension as they made the pictures. The doctor in the X-ray room studied the pictures when they were developed. He didn't speak to us, and when I asked what the pictures showed he said, "Your son's neck is broken." I knew that such an injury was nearly always fatal.

I asked, "Is there a chance for him to live?"

"Oh, yes," he answered.

When Hentz left the X-ray room he was taken to a semi-private room already occupied by a young policeman whose leg had been crushed. Hentz was not taken off the ambulance stretcher because the doctor didn't want him moved. He did not seem to be suffering; but before long a nurse came and gave him a hypodermic.

The orthopedic surgeon was in the operating room and couldn't see Hentz, but he sent his associate to examine him. I wondered what it meant when he asked Hentz to move his legs. Hentz couldn't move them. The doctor asked him to move his right arm. Hentz couldn't; but he could move his left arm a little, though he could not feel the pin pricks the doctor made over his body. I didn't know the meaning of the pin. How many times later on I would watch doctors pin pricking my son's body and cry out to God to let him feel it!

The hours of waiting dragged on. The surgeon was still in the operating room. Friends started gathering in the hall outside the room. Hentz was sleeping now from the shot, and he looked restful enough even though sandbags were packed around his neck and head to prevent him from making any movement of the neck. After a while the young doctor returned and called Fred and me into the hall. We walked a few feet up the hall away from the crowd of people. By this time rumors had spread that Hentz's neck was not broken, but dislocated in a not too serious way. We were eager to believe the good news.

The doctor began to talk. "I hate to tell you this because I am not your doctor, but Dr. Hill is still operating and he thinks you should know your son's condition. His spinal cord is severed—or nearly severed. It will be a miracle if he pulls out of this."

I had a horrible feeling of being violently swept into swirling black waters and of suffocating. Fred was so pale that I was afraid he was going to faint. I saw the exit nearby. People were looking at us, and I wanted to get out in the fresh air. We walked out onto the lawn and stood in the shade of a crepe myrtle tree. Neither of us spoke.

After a long silence Fred said: "Well, there are a lot of things he can do even if he is crippled. With his mind, nothing will stop him." I knew he was trying to reassure me, and perhaps himself.

I said: "The doctor does not think Hentz will live. That is what he meant. He meant it would be a miracle if he lived."

Fred turned even whiter than he had been. "No. He could not have meant that."

I wanted to believe him, but I knew better. We looked toward the hospital and saw the young doctor approaching us. I had to know what he meant when he had talked to us in the hall, so I asked him.

"Mrs. Houser, it nearly kills me to have to tell you; but if your son lives it will be a miracle. It might be twelve hours, or eighteen—maybe twenty-four. We don't see how he can live."

I suppose every mother has wondered, at some time, how

she would react to such tragic news. All of us probably have such moments of projected fear and torment. I had always thought it was the one verdict I couldn't face. I had believed that my heart would stop, or that I would go mad. Nothing like that happened.

We didn't cry. One sob—no more—shook Fred violently. I hoped I would wake as if from a horrible nightmare—no longer to see the man sprinkling fertilizer on the grass; the many people panting as they climbed the long front steps with flowers in their arms; the quiet young doctor anxiously standing there to know if we needed his help; the nurses and internes moving swiftly, efficiently back and forth in the long hall.

I don't know how long we stood there.

Later that summer the crepe myrtle tree was cut down. Fred said he was glad because he hated it. From then until now two years have elapsed. Our son still lives. So does the crepe myrtle tree, which has sprouted anew from its roots.

It bloomed gloriously last summer.

CHAPTER TWO

It was 4:00 P.M. on that first day when they came to take Hentz to the operating room. As the elevator door closed between Hentz and us, I felt as though the world had been suddenly split in two and that if I advanced one step I would fall into a bottomless chasm. I didn't know then that an elevator door would shut me off from him for twelve operations in less than two years. Hentz had grinned at us and joked as he was whisked away—as he would grin on all those other occasions.

Dr. Hill made arrangements for us to occupy a room on the floor that Hentz was on. Every few minutes after Hentz was brought from the operating room I would go to stand outside my son's room, bow my head as I stood there in the hall, and ask God to help all of us—especially Hentz. I was afraid to go inside the room. I wanted to see Hentz so very much, but the strangeness and the stillness terrified me. I could only press my face against the door that separated us and hope that God knew our need.

Later that first night Dr. Hill came to the room Fred and I occupied. He fumbled for words and seemed to dread the task before him. Slowly he explained that the spinal cord was a part of the body that did not regenerate itself. Any injury

6

done to it was permanent. He was trying to tell us not to hope that Hentz would ever use his hands or arms or legs again. In fact, he was trying to say more: he didn't want us to hope too much that Hentz would live. He told us that they put tongs into Hentz's skull in the operating room, and that they put as much weight on them as possible in an effort to pull the jammed vertebrae apart. He said an operation was not indicated. We know now that he meant that an operation would have been fatal.

I felt more composed than during the afternoon, and was conscious of trying to think the thing through. I asked him if he'd ever known anyone to live with an injury as serious as Hentz's.

He said, "I've known one person."

"If anybody else can do it, Hentz can too," I declared. Perhaps that was the beginning of the long, uphill fight.

I couldn't believe that a person as vital as Hentz could be stilled so suddenly. Why, he was life itself! I remembered all the things he had done during the last year in high school. He was president of the senior class, president of the student council, president of the Key Club, lieutenant governor of the Georgia Key Clubs, and president of the Youth Fellowship of the Methodist Church; assistant Scout Master; he was on the debating team, and on the annual staff; he was a cheerleader. He was planning to go to Georgia Tech in the fall. He was destined for great things in the world. He had always been the kind of boy who accepted leadership naturally and modestly. Could it be that this accident would cancel all these prospects? I couldn't accept such a wasteful probability.

After Hentz lived through the first twelve hours, the doctors said, "Twenty-four hours." Then it was thirty-six, then seventy-two. They were astonished. Medical knowledge had said that he would die.

During those first days we chartered a plane to Atlanta to bring a neurosurgeon to see Hentz. He advised against an operation because Hentz's condition was too critical. He told us that Hentz had a chance to live, but that he would never recover the use of his limbs. He was the first doctor who held out any hope for his life.

I asked the Atlanta doctor what we should do about telling Hentz. Did he think the patient should be told? He said it was a question that had never been settled, that there had been much argument about it, and that we would have to decide for ourselves, with the help of our minister. I knew that I could never tell my only child that the doctors said he would never use his arms and legs again, because I didn't believe it. Love overrides all other decisions, and I knew I would not stand by his bed and watch all his hopes and dreams needlessly die out of his eyes. Nor would I permit any other person to tell him. I have never regretted that decision.

Hentz had lived past the extremely critical period. He looked strong and talked sensibly. Dr. Hill had called in a doctor of internal medicine, and I was waiting in the hall outside Hentz's door when he came out after his first examination. Because the doctor did not look worried or downhearted, I asked, "Well, what do you think?" His answer sent me back to the edge of the dreaded chasm.

He rapped his fingers with his stethoscope as he said, "I've never seen a blacker picture."

From that moment, and for a long time afterward, I dreaded that doctor with a fear that was almost physical. When I knew he was in the hospital I was filled with anxiety. Whenever he went into my son's room, I left that wing of the building until I was certain he'd gone. I conquered this feeling, of course, and all of us now feel a devotion to him that is close to reverence.

The following day, which was Sunday, six or seven hundred people came to the hospital to inquire about Hentz, and to assure us that they were thinking of us and praying for us. Their concern was one of the greatest helps we had. During those first critical nights close friends of ours slept all over the hospital—or tried to sleep. Some were in the X-ray waiting rooms, and some on screened porches; others were in halls, vacant rooms, and every available spot. People throughout our entire section of the state were deeply concerned. A neighboring town had to put on extra telephone operators to take care of the calls.

On that first Sunday afternoon the nurse suddenly came out of Hentz's room, hurried through the crowds in the halls, and made her way to a telephone where she called Dr. Hill for oxygen. He came quickly and assured me that the situation was not as alarming as the nurse had indicated. Hentz's breathing had been affected because the diaphragm muscles were paralyzed. Though this crisis passed, I had been badly frightened. I wanted very much to cry with relief. However, many of our friends were there, and I wanted them to think I was strong. After working my way to the edge of the long screened porch, I turned my back to the people, and began to cry silently. In a moment I felt a man's strong arm around my shoulder, and I could feel it trembling. I didn't dare to look at the man lest he see that I was crying.

In a gentle voice that was choked with emotion, he said: "Try not to worry. Hentz is not going to die. I know that. He

is not going to die! If I were an eloquent man I could tell
you how I know. I prayed all night, and I have definite
assurance that Hentz is going to be all right."

I turned to look at my kind neighbor, because by now I
knew he was crying too. Yet his face was a portrait of reassurance. It held a radiance undimmed by tears. I felt strangely
quiet and comforted. His face bore testimony that his
prayers had been heard. Many, many times, when Hentz
was very low, and we were gripped with nameless terror,
we thought of this good man's words and gained fresh hope.
Though he probably doesn't know what his words meant to
us, after each discouraging report Fred would say: "But
Ed says it will be all right. Ed says he *knows*."

That Sunday all of the churches in our home town had
special prayer services for Hentz, and the young people
gathered for prayer. I was told that the churches in Macon
had special services too. We have many friends there, and
we thought it unusually good of them to do this for a young
boy not of their community. The young people, especially,
were trusting and confident that their prayers would be
answered. I well know how earnestly they prayed, for Hentz
too had joined his young friends to pray for a high-school
senior who had drowned at the lake during the previous
year. Hentz had been with the boy and had left him, laughing and talking on the float, to cross the road to the country
store to get a bottled drink. By the time he returned to the
lake, George had drowned. I'll never forget Hentz's face as
he walked toward me in our yard. He said that people were
still diving looking for George, and that they planned to
use grappling hooks. He came home before the hooks were
put into use, and went to his room to learn from the encyclo-

pedia how long a person could remain under water and be revived. I knew that he stayed in his room to ask God to spare George's life. Later, I wondered what he felt when George was pronounced dead. My answer came as I watched his face at George's funeral. Though Hentz and his young friends were certain that their prayers would be answered, even after George's death they retained their faith in divine Providence. I have often wondered since if any doubt or bitterness is ever felt by Hentz's friends because of his pro- longed illness. I hope they have patience together with their faith.

The Thursday following the accident stands out in my memory clear and sharp. The events leading up to this day are all jumbled together like leaves in a whirlwind. I can still see the nurses as they worked with great efficiency and tension; every line and expression of the tight-lipped doctors is indelibly preserved in my memory; and I shall never forget the terrifying consultations between the doctors.

I sat in a chair in one corner of the room and watched as strangers came and went, doing their part to help my boy. Someone was always telling me that I should rest and spare myself. Though I didn't need rest, it was easier sometimes to yield than to resist, so I was led to my room down the hall to lie down. Before long one of Fred's cousins, Francis Nunn, who is also one of our closest friends, came to my room. He said, "You had better go to Hentz." Moving like something wooden, I walked beside him and out of the little room.

Suddenly, as if it were a pronouncement that had to be made as quickly as possible, he said, "Hentz is dying." I could not speak, and in a moment he continued: "For a while it seemed that the end would be at any minute, but he is putting up a terrific fight. With his strong constitution he won't give up easily."

Even amid the wild noises in my head and the whirling, I knew it was more than Hentz's constitution that wouldn't give up easily. We took a few more steps, and the unreality of it gripped me again. Could he have meant my son? I remember saying silently: "Keep on fighting, Hentz. There will be help. Don't stop a second! I'm coming, and we'll think of something!"

I entered Hentz's room. Fred was on one side of the bed and one of our close friends, Ruth Rogers, was opposite him. This friend had known and loved Hentz all his life, and lavished some of the love she'd had for the children that didn't come to her, on him. She called him a silly name she'd had for him when he was a little boy, and as she fanned him to help him breathe she'd murmur some of the tender things she used to say long ago. Fred was fanning too, and between heart-breaking gasps Hentz begged them to fan him so that he could breathe. It was unreal, and yet so tragically real. He was fighting valiantly for life itself.

I watched in unbelief for a while. Ed had said Hentz would not die, and I had prayed so hard. I had believed Ed and had had faith, but Hentz was dying anyhow.

Then I decided to pray. It seemed that medical science could not help him now. I sat in a chair at the foot of the bed, and amid all the agony and heartbreak I began to pray. I've forgotten the exact words, but not the urgency and commitment with which I called upon God. I prayed more fervently than I ever had before. After a while a very strange sensation of peace and quiet came over me. It was a peace that defies a reasonable explanation, because nothing in the room contributed to it. Almost as if awaking from a trance I arose from the chair, walked to the lavatory, and washed my face in ice water.

Suddenly I heard Ruth demanding that the nurse get a doctor.

The nurse replied, "I can get a house doctor, but today is Thursday and the other doctors are out."

Ruth was indignant, and persisted. "We don't want a house doctor. We want one of Hentz's doctors, and we want one quick!"

The nurse hesitated, and in her hesitation I could read all the hopelessness that the doctors and nurses felt. She was probably wondering if calling doctors could help the situation. As she left the room, she said in a doubtful tone that she would see if she could find any of them.

In a very few minutes we had five doctors! I prayed again that God would give them the wisdom to do something to save Hentz's life. Thirty minutes passed before they came out of the room. Dr. Hill was grim and furious.

"Hentz ought to get better now. What happened was inexcusable!" I don't know what he meant and what was inexcusable, but the kidneys had been blocked all day, and probably during the night. When that was corrected, Hentz rallied. If we had not called the doctors when we did, it would have been too late. Very early I learned that we had an obligation to be alert to changing circumstances requiring emergency care.

We call that day Black Thursday, but I shall remember it for another reason also. It was on that day that God showed me His great power and His great love. There have been many times when I have prayed, since then, without visible result. I believe that on such occasions there was some lack on my part. In spite of the thousands of heartbreaks, the days of anxiety, disappointment, and uncertainty, I've never lost the conviction that God is personally interested in me, and hears my prayers.

A cousin of mine, a Presbyterian minister, was at the hospital on that Black Thursday. Something he said has been of great help. The things that have helped us are not new and startling, but old truths that we've heard all our lives. Hearing them repeated by someone who so completely believed them made them sound new and wonderful. As my cousin was leaving he turned to me and said: "Don't ever forget this: All things work together for good for those who love the Lord." I found myself repeating those twelve words all during the day and night. I could bear the strain if I knew the ultimate end would be good.

When I started writing this I thought I ought to study and read and make the things I believe sound profound and learned. I decided against that because it would be false and dishonest, as well as impossible. What I believe is so simple and uncluttered by doctrines and creeds that any child can understand it. *I believe that God is all-powerful.* This simple faith has been the force that has kept me going during my ordeal. It has done for our family more than that. We don't live just one day at a time, bearing the trials with a martyr's patience. We actually look forward to the future. We don't pretend to enjoy the days when Hentz is suffering most. Those days are difficult for all of us, but we get through them, knowing that better ones will come; and they always do. I don't know the specific nature of my husband's beliefs or what Hentz believes. It is enough for me to know that they *do* believe.

The problems presented themselves in such quick succession during those first days and weeks that they must have exhausted our doctors. One of the most serious problems was the actual care of Hentz. We could not move him because his neck was not set, and turning him could have been fatal. The hospital did not have an orthopedic frame which would permit him to be turned without actually being moved. Fred and I did not know the grave seriousness of this situation. For one week Hentz lay in one position, while the nurses tried to massage his back with alcohol by slipping their hands under him. After he lived a week the doctors knew he would have to have his position changed. The anesthesiologist knew of a hospital in Augusta that had some extra orthopedic beds. He told us that such a bed would eliminate pressure sores, and we didn't know they could cause death until Dr. Taft, the doctor of internal medicine, said: "Bed sores will probably be the cause of your son's death. It is impossible to move him and there is no way to prevent the sores." It was a hideous thought. Hentz was so careful of his person, and such a fate was unthinkable. When we learned that there was a bed that would enable Hentz to change position, we were very happy.

The problem of getting the bed as quickly as possible arose, but it was not a problem very long. Francis Nunn, who was at the hospital, said he would go to Augusta immediately to get the bed. Though several trucks are used in his farm supply warehouse, he wouldn't wait for one of his trucks to be brought to Macon from Perry. Instead he went downtown in Macon and bought a truck for the special purpose of making the trip! When he returned from Augusta he resold the truck to the original owner.

Hentz was carefully transferred to the orthopedic frame, which was called a Foster bed, and turned on his stomach.

Immediately he seemed to feel more comfortable. He was in so much less pain that the doctors and nurses didn't want to turn him back again. He remained face down for forty-eight hours. When he was turned back again I was sickened by what I saw. I felt a strange mixture of love, sympathy, and revulsion as I looked at his swollen face with its distended eyes. Above the eyes that mirrored pain instead of the customary mirth, his forehead was a dark, bleeding mass of hideous blisters. There was nothing in that face that told me it belonged to my son. His neck was swollen until there was little demarcation between the jawline and shoulders. His tongue and lips were swollen until his speech was unintelligible. I remember praying that I would be able to look upon my son's face and be assured that it would quickly assume its natural appearance. The terrible pain was so much easier when Hentz looked natural.

The damage was caused by the weight of his body, plus the added weight of the traction, all of which was supported by his forehead, which was pressed hard upon a heavy canvas strap. There was an ugly pressure sore on his sacrum caused by the lack of turning in bed during the first week.

This shocking experience was my introduction to pressure sores.

One morning, a few days after the accident, a friend came to my room in the hospital and said that a Mr. Sanders wanted to see me. I didn't recall knowing anyone by that name, but I told my friend to ask him in. A nice-looking man came into the room. He said: "I'm B. B. Sanders, with the Vocational Rehabilitation Department. I heard about your son's accident, and want to talk to you about a rehabilitation program for him, when he is able to be dismissed from this hospital."

He saw my distress and confusion, and continued: "In New York there is great work being done for people like your son. He can be taught to do many things for himself."

I had no idea what he was talking about, and I didn't want to discuss it. I had always associated "rehabilitation" with delinquents and alcoholics, and I didn't want to think that Hentz would have to be sent away somewhere to learn to do simple tasks for himself. At this time I knew that one day Hentz would be well and strong, and would not need the things Mr. Sanders had in mind. He was an understanding man, and said: "It is probably too early to think about it now, but I will keep up with Hentz, and keep informed as to his progress. When the time comes, we'll help."

I didn't think any more about the visit, because there were too many other things to think about. Little did I know, then, what this man and the vocational program would mean to us.

During the week a neurosurgeon from Johns Hopkins examined Hentz. I was not then in the room, and never inquired of Fred as to the prognosis. As the doctor left the room and saw me standing in the hall, he said, "High fever and mental confusion are dreaded symptoms." Immediately Hentz's fever soared to 106 degrees. He said strange things to me, such as begging me to let his ninety-pound dog, Dan, out of the dresser drawer. Once again the doctors said there was not a glimmer of hope.

From that time on I decided to ask fewer questions. My ignorance of many phases of this early experience is the result of this decision. I knew the doctors could not honestly say anything encouraging, and discouraging reports only frightened me and destroyed the calm I was struggling to attain. Hope, even a frail hope, can sometimes assume majestic proportions and lead us on to triumph where the hopelessness would speed us along the road to defeat.

Crisis followed crisis those first days and weeks, yet with each crisis something occurred to strengthen our faith. When everything seemed darkest we would be lifted up by one friend's faith and another's love.

Whenever I felt the terror of being whirled to the edge of the black chasm, some inner calm always came to my rescue before I fell into the bottomless pit. From somewhere phrases and sentences like, *O ye of little faith,* and, *Whatsoever ye shall ask the Father in my name he will give it you,* labored their way into my mind and heart. It was then that I knew that faith and prayer were steadying me.

CHAPTER THREE

Monday after the accident we received a telephone message
from a Mr. Van Diviere of Brunswick. He prefaced what he
had to say with the explanation that he was no crank. He said
that he knew we would get many messages from cranks and
fanatics, but that he was neither. Then he told us that he
and his wife had been through a similar ordeal with their
only son. Their son had been nineteen at the time, and a
student at the University of Georgia when his neck was
broken in an automobile accident.

Mr. and Mrs. Van Diviere had seen an account of Hentz's
accident in the Atlanta papers, and were anxious to tell us
about a new drug which effected a cure for their son when
all seemed lost. While her son had lingered between living
and dying, she had noticed an article in a newspaper about
a new drug, not then released from the laboratory, that
might give hope to victims of severed spinal cords. The
article said that the drug had never been tried on human
beings, but that it had caused cats to regain muscular function
after having had their spinal cords severed. Mrs. Van Diviere
had begged her son's doctor to try it. He had scoffed at the
idea. She had gone to Atlanta and implored the doctors there.

19

They had also refused. Then she had gone to the man who
discovered the drug's possibilities. He had said he did not
know that it would benefit her boy, but he knew it would
do no harm. There had been nothing to lose because no other
hope had been offered. The drug had been flown to Georgia
and administered to the boy several months after his accident.
In a few weeks he had begun to move muscles that had long
been inactive; he had begun to have feeling in his nerveless
body. When it was possible to move him, he had been flown
to New York, where he received treatment at the Institute of
Physical Medicine and Rehabilitation. In less than a year he
had gone back to the university. Mr. and Mrs. Van Diviere
gave Dr. Taft the name and address of the doctor in Chicago,
and he called immediately. The first bottle of Pyromen was
flown to Macon one week after Hentz was hurt. We felt
confident that Hentz's recovery would be more rapid than
the other boy's had been because we had an earlier start.

A few days later the Van Divieres drove to Macon with
their son. They were especially anxious to see our doctors.
They had learned much from their experience, and wanted
to share that knowledge with us.

When Mr. and Mrs. Van Diviere knocked on Hentz's door
and I opened it, I didn't have to ask who they were. There
was a light of victory shining in their eyes. I felt toward them
as a new recruit in the army must feel toward an old colonel
who has fought and been wounded in many battles. They
said that their son, Charles, was outside in the car and would
be in later.

An orderly had put several chairs on a side porch for the
visitors, the doctors, and Fred and me. A consciousness of
the duties of a hostess made me overcome my fear of Dr.
Taft. I sat down on the porch with our guests and our doctors.

As Dr. Taft talked to the Van Divieres I sensed his goodness and his interest in my son. He didn't seem to feel as hopeless about Hentz as he had earlier.

The Van Divieres brought all the charts that were kept during Charles's hospitalization. They were so enthusiastic and intelligent that I saw immediately that our doctors were interested.

I saw Mrs. Van Diviere smiling, and as I followed her glance toward the doorway I saw a tall, slender young man walking toward us with the aid of Canadian canes. My heart sank. I thought they had said he was cured! This was not what I considered a cure. I wanted more than this for my son! Mrs. Van Diviere assured us that Charles would be without the canes in a little while. The doctors in New York had said it was just a matter of his ankle getting stronger.

We had told Hentz that Charles was coming to see him. We hoped that meeting someone who'd been through a similar experience would help him. But I couldn't let Charles go in using his canes! Hentz wouldn't want to think he would have to walk with canes a year from now. I asked Charles if he could walk without them, and he said he could if he held his father's arm. I went into Hentz's room first and told him that the Van Divieres had come to see him. Charles and his father entered the room together and advanced toward the bed, the boy trying to appear as though holding his father's arm was from affection and not necessity. Hentz was lying on his face on the Foster bed and would have been able to see Charles's feet and the canes.

The Van Divieres told me to turn deaf ears to people who said Hentz couldn't recover. They said they thought our choice of doctors was a wise one, and advised us to do everything they advised—and to have a faith that never wavered.

Mrs. Van Diviere told me of the wonderful work she saw being done at the Institute of Physical Medicine and Rehabilitation, and expressed her hope that we would get Hentz there as quickly as possible.

Fred and I followed the Van Divieres to their car when they were ready to leave. We wanted to hear everything they had to say because they had been where we were then, and had won a very happy victory. The gratitude and happiness they felt showed in every word they spoke and every move they made, and their strength and belief that Hentz would live and walk were transmitted to my eager heart. As they drove away they promised to come back. They have kept that promise. They have been with us during all the operations Hentz had in Georgia. They were never too busy with their own affairs to drive across the state to be with us. Mrs. Van Diviere wrote wonderful letters telling me of the faith she had that Hentz would recover. She seemed to sense when a telephone call from her would help through a bad night.

I hope these people know, to a small extent, what their help and encouragement have meant to us. They taught us to grit our teeth and *fight*.

The long days dragged by. I still had the room at the hospital two weeks after the accident. Hentz was still holding on. He wasn't gaining very much strength, but at least he was alive.

In my room at the hospital the password was—Hope. If anyone knocked on the door we would ask if they were optimists or pessimists. Only the optimists gained entrance. Sometimes there would be fifteen or twenty of us packed in the small space.

My sister, Julia Bolin who lives in Arizona, called as soon

as she received the telegram about Hentz's accident. I tried very hard to sound brave over the telephone, and when she asked me if I wanted her to come I wouldn't tell her how desperately I needed her. She had visited us only recently, and I knew that she was needed at her home with her three small boys and her husband, and that the trip was a long and expensive one. It was with a feeling of loss and sadness that I replaced the receiver on its hook. She had the kind of strength that I needed. She was a year older than I, and when we were children she protected and mothered me with a love seldom found between sisters. There was never any jealousy—just her determination that I should not be hurt physically or in any other way. And for practical reasons I could not tell her to come! I felt more helpless than I did as a child, and needed her to stand between me and the whirl-wind that might at any time sweep me to the brink of the gaping chasm.

The day following our telephone conversation, a friend of Hentz's, Charles Bledsoe, and I were sitting on a bench near the front entrance. Listlessly I watched a trim, well dressed woman paying a cab driver who had deposited her bags on the porch of the hospital. I remember thinking for a fleeting second that the woman was pretty and capable-looking. I was too deep in thought to notice her features. Then I saw Charles leap to his feet, and cry out, "That's Julia!" The front door opened and she came toward me. With a flood of relief, dependence, and a knowledge that somehow she could make things better, I ran to her. All she could say was, "I caught the first plane."

We had a cot put in my room for Sister. Knowing that she was close by in the darkness was very comforting. When I couldn't sleep I could tell her how frightened I was. After my strength came back and drove the fright away, she rejoiced with me. We were as we had been when we were children.

A few days after Sister arrived, Dr. Hill told me that he thought it wise for me to give up the room at the hospital and go back home. He said: "It will be difficult for you to go back to a house that you left when everything was good and right; but you will have to go back sometime, and now is the time."

I was near exhaustion when I got home. I was afraid of the house, and wouldn't look up as I walked in the door. I was afraid of the familiar; now it had become alien. The familiar was now the smell and the noises of the hospital where Hentz was fighting to live. When I climbed the stairs I thought: I will go in Hentz's room. I will force myself to do it. I walked through the door, and turned suddenly and walked back into the hall. I wasn't strong enough for that —not yet. I stood in the hall thinking: I must go in the room now, and not let the fear of what it will do to me keep me out. If I don't go in now it will be more difficult tomorrow. The next day it will be still more difficult. I must conquer this thing now. Now! I must touch the things Hentz touched. I must sit in the chairs and lie on the bed. I must sit at his desk. I must believe that he will do these things too—some day.

I turned again and started into my son's room. At first I held my head down—afraid to behold the walls that separated his room from the rest of the house; afraid to look at the bed where he'd rested and dreamed dreams; afraid to see the model plane he'd put together with fingers agile and sure; afraid to look at the shoes that were scuffed when his feet were strong and running from one excitement to the other. I was weak and afraid, and as I stood there I prayed to God to give me courage. The courage came and I walked into the room. I touched everything. I fell across his bed, and I read some of his scribbling on papers on the desk. I don't know how long I remained in the room, but when I left I was not afraid. I had won a battle, and I knew that I would never have this particular battle to fight again. I knew that I would be afraid again, and that I would be hurt, but not in the same way.

That first night at home set the pattern for so many that would follow. I went to my room to go to bed; but sleep wouldn't come until I talked to God about our burdens and asked Him to make things right. No matter how difficult the day, I always knew that if I could be alone in my home and talk it over with God the outlook would seem better. So many people have asked me how I've found the strength to go on and on. Love, and the faith and belief of others have helped; but if I had to name the one thing that has made me carry on, and not miss a day because of sickness, fatigue, or grief, I would say it was those hours. The house was so strangely quiet, and my need so terribly great, that I could get closer to God then than I ever had before.

CHAPTER FOUR

After the first night at home, I left Perry about eight o'clock in the morning to return to the hospital. Fred had agreed to leave Hentz, when I arrived, and to go back to his office. Filled with dread and eager anticipation, I walked down the hall to Room 231. Was Hentz worse? Maybe he was better! When I slowly opened the door and saw Fred and the nurse and Hentz, I felt relief flood over me.

Hentz was asleep, and I whispered to Fred: "Have you had any breakfast? I haven't. Let's go to the snack bar and get something." It was good to be with him in the crowded snack bar, and to talk about everything that had happened during the night. Fred never complained, and always tried to picture each event in the best possible light. After breakfast, as he was leaving to go back to his office for the first time since the accident, he turned and said: "Take care of everything. I'll be thinking about you." I knew how difficult it would be for him to go to his office and try to begin again where he had left off when Hentz was hurt.

That first day without Fred seemed endless, and I could hardly wait until seven-thirty or eight o'clock when he and his sisters, Leonora and Louise, would come back. Leonora said she would bring her car and leave it for Fred to return to Perry the next morning. She, Louise, Charles Bledsoe, and I would return to Perry in our car so that I would have it to use the next morning.

With very slight variations the events of that first day were duplicated hundreds of times. There were the early-morning anxiety and anticipation; there was breakfast with Fred in the crowded snack bar; there were Louise and Leonora, my mother and Fred's mother, steady and loving, suffering when we suffered and rejoicing when we rejoiced; there was Charles—until he went away to college. Through it all there was hope.

We had special nurses all the time; but they had to leave the room many times during the day, and we didn't want Hentz ever to feel that he was alone and unattended. Fred was very weary, and for a few nights during the early part of Hentz's hospitalization good friends insisted that he get a night's sleep in a bed while they took turns sleeping on the little cot. They knew and appreciated our desire to be with Hentz, who was often so nervous that he had difficulty sleeping. At those times it helped him to know a good friend was nearby. They would laugh and talk with him about hunting, fishing, sports, and other things he was interested in. Even though we never asked anyone to stay, there were always more generous offers than we had need of.

Hospital personnel, friends, and acquaintances did everything possible to spare Hentz unnecessary discomfort. His young friends showed a devotion of a kind we'd never seen.

Charles Bledsoe, who had finished school with Hentz, began going to the hospital every morning; and before I realized it I was depending on him for many things. He was extremely capable, and his personality made him a great asset both in the sickroom and outside it. He is an ageless sort of young man, and as much of a comfort to me as he was a friend to Hentz. He is interesting and clever. He pretends to dislike humanity; but I think he knows that we all know he is something of a "softie." His friends are fortunate indeed, and their number is greater than he would admit. Charles is quick with repartee, and he and Hentz complement each other because each tries to outwit the other. I marveled at the keenness of their minds, and remembered the pride I'd known as I listened to them debate together a few short weeks before at the district meet. I was pleased, but not surprised, when they won the debate.

If a pessimistic visitor came to the hospital, Charles would grit his teeth; and after they had left he would growl, "I hate them!" He was one of the few people closely associated with Hentz who did not give up hope. If he'd had no other virtues, his optimism alone would have forever endeared him to me.

I don't quite know how it all came about, but I accepted the fact that Charles would go to the hospital with me every morning. After I gave up my room in the hospital and spent my nights in Perry, I would stop by for him when I left for Macon. It was good to have him for company on the ride. He could always convince me that things were better than they actually were. Hentz always brightened up when Charles came in.

Turning Hentz on the Foster bed was delicate business because of his neck not being set, and Dr. Hill had to be there each time to supervise the operation. Charles took charge of all the preliminary details of the procedure such as getting the sheets and clipping one over the thick layer of foam rubber that padded the canvas bed. It took a minimum of five persons to turn Hentz. Two were required on each side of the bed and one person had to hold his head firmly so that it would not move and cause further injury to the spinal cord.

When Hentz was turned on his stomach, the ulcer on his back had to be cleansed and dressed. Dr. Hill showed Charles what to do, for Charles always assisted him and the nurse. Later he assisted the nurse, and when there was no nurse on duty he did it alone.

When Hentz was first hurt he wanted to have the record player going all the time. Charles was the self-appointed disc jockey. Knowing of Hentz's need for music, friends sent hundreds of records and albums. Some of those records recall all the anxiety and suspense of those early months, and I cannot bear to hear them now. Charles said later that, regardless of where he was, when he heard one of those songs he would suddenly be transported to Room 231 of the Macon Hospital. He smelled again all the medicines and felt all the old tensions. Until he said that, I hadn't known he had been under tension.

Hentz had a corner room, and at the end of the hall, just outside his door, was a window. Charles and I fixed this little spot for our quarters. The hospital was wonderful about all these things, and permitted us to do anything that added to our comfort or peace of mind. Under the window we had the roll-away bed that Fred slept on. We had tables and chairs and flowers and books. Here we entertained the callers who came when Hentz was trying to rest, and occasionally we caught little cat naps.

Charles's upsetting trait of seeing through my pretenses and little defenses made him know when I was particularly worried about something. No matter how hard I tried to

conceal some new fear or change, Charles would detect it.
I always felt better after I had confided in him. He never
showed any signs of squeamishness, regardless of the task
he was doing for Hentz. He was gentle always; and unless
Hentz was too sick Charles always found something amusing
about the job at hand. He was so competent that the doctors
had as much confidence in him as we did. He attended several of Hentz's operations. He made molds for casts, and did
many things that saved time for the doctors. It was during
this time that he knew he would become a doctor. He is
now at Vanderbilt University taking his premedical course.

Charles has been through so many dark places with us
that there is an understanding between us that is almost
eerie. We miss him terribly when he is away at school; and
I know of no happier moment than when I open the door
and find him smiling there. Recently I was upstairs and
heard someone knock. Charles was not expected to be at
home, as it was not a week end or a holiday; but as soon as
I heard the knock I ran downstairs and called his name before
I opened the door. He said, "How did you know?" Until he
asked I hadn't realized that I couldn't possibly have known.
No therapy we have ever tried works the wonders with
Hentz that a visit from Charles does. If Hentz has had the
bad news that he must undergo surgery again, he is glum
until Charles makes light of it. He teases Hentz about his
clumsiness in hitting his head on the bottom of the lake; but
beneath all the lightness and laughing we know how much
he cares. It is a comforting thought.

Felton Norwood is another young boy whose interest and
desire to help have never wavered. He is two years younger
than Hentz and Charles. Usually that much difference in
ages among the very young leaves a gap that makes perfect

understanding impossible. It wasn't that way with Felton because he is a most adaptable person. Like Charles, his willingness to do everything possible for Hentz's comfort was uppermost in his mind.

When Hentz had to be turned on his stomach on the Foster bed, the pressure on his face was torturous. Because of the damage to his forehead, the cheeks and chin had to support the upper part of his body, and they would swell painfully. At those times, if Felton was at the hospital, he would lie on the floor on his back and bathe Hentz's eyes and stuff minute pieces of foam rubber in places around his face to ease the pressure. He would talk to Hentz to keep his mind off the pain and discomfort.

Felton also assisted with the care of the ulcer on Hentz's back. Like Charles, there was nothing to be done that he minded doing. Both boys assisted in many tasks even though we had three nurses. The nurses appreciated their help and intelligence. Though Felton had a job during the summer, he went to the hospital at every opportunity. Somehow he was there nearly every night. Though he was still in high school, he too made up his mind that he would be a doctor. He is now at the University of Georgia doing his premed work.

Felton calls me Mother, which is short for Mother Bird. Years ago Fred started calling me Mother Bird—for some foolish reason which I've forgotten—and several of the people I love best of all call me that. It pleases me so much to have Felton rush into the house, breathless over something that has pleased him, and say, "Mother, just let me tell you what happened!"

Charles and Felton are modest about their records at school, but if I insist they will admit that they are making excellent grades. Felton will complete his work at the

university in two years, and he and Charles will enter the
Emory School of Medicine in the fall of 1955. We have
a peculiar pride in them because we feel that they are partly
our own.

Not all of the young company and companions on the
floor under the Foster bed were masculine. Mary Jane Pettus
assumed the task of bathing Hentz's face as her very special
job, and after she came to Perry for a prolonged visit Felton
had to occupy himself some other way.

Mary Jane and Hentz had been dating off and on for years
when she visited a cousin in Perry. She is from Birmingham,
Alabama, and usually visited two or three times each year.
She and Hentz corresponded; and just before he was hurt I
think the spasmodic romance had become more serious. She
spent most of that first summer in Perry, went to the hospital
with Charles and me, and stayed until we came back at
night. Mothers are usually quite critical of the girls their
sons admire, but Mary Jane would have pleased the most
critical mother. Her manner was as lovely as her features,
and she had a poise seldom found in such a young person.
She was good for all of us, and I found myself leaning on her
many times for added strength. She concealed any feelings
of distress so well that I was surprised to learn later that the
strain had made her extremely nervous.

After Dr. Hill had supervised the turning of Hentz, and
other tasks had been completed, Mary Jane would come back
into the room and lie on the floor under the bed. She had
little dimples at each corner of her mouth, and she smiled
up at Hentz during her ministrations. I used to sit and watch
her, trying to imagine what she was thinking—and what
Hentz was thinking. Surely there was nothing romantic about

the situation. How could a young girl do what she was doing? I felt so humbly grateful to her for trying to make a terrible situation seem less terrible for my son. I thought that what she was doing was beautiful—and I was constantly torn between beauty and sadness. They were everywhere.

Later in the evening Dr. Taft would make his call, and it was always while Mary Jane was lying on the floor. The doctor never saw her at her task without telling me how wonderful he thought it was, and how beautiful she was. Every night he said he wanted to bring a camera on the next visit, but he never did. Mary Jane acted as though bathing the hurt boy's eyes and face with ice water was the most exciting thing she'd ever done.

Although I never could understand how the visits at the hospital could be anything other than prolonged suspense, the lives of three young people were changed because of them. Before Hentz's accident Mary Jane had planned to continue with voice lessons, but after spending the summer with Hentz in the hospital she decided to enter the nursing profession. She was to receive her Bachelor of Science degree from the University of Alabama in the spring of 1955.

The weeks piled up until I was afraid to count them. I recalled that Mrs. Van Diviere had said that her son started getting the feeling back in his hands and legs at four and one half months. When Hentz had been hurt that long and was no better, I became especially anxious. Mrs. Van Diviere told me that Hentz would probably take longer because his neck was not set for many weeks and Charles's was set immediately. But Hentz had been getting Pyromen so long —so much earlier than the other boy. I knew that the

second month would show some change—the next week—
the week after that. And so it went. Hoping, hoping, praying
and waiting.

I dreaded to have Hentz ask the date because I feared
that the flight of time might diminish his hope. I know now
that he never doubted that he would recover fully, and
that that faith kept him in good spirits.

One day when I arrived at the hospital in Macon for
my day's stay, the floor supervisor met me in the hall. She
caught my hands in hers, and there were tears shining in
her eyes. I wasn't frightened because I could see that they
were tears of happiness.

"Hentz moved his legs! His knees are moving! Just think,
he can move!" She could say no more.

"Oh, how good! I'm so thankful! I knew he would some
day, but it has taken so long!" I don't suppose I have ever
known a happier moment.

When I reached the room Fred was beaming. Hentz's
nurse was nearly beside herself. Hentz said he'd never heard
such a commotion about a knee moving. He said: "Why
shouldn't it move? That's what it's supposed to do." He
tried to pretend that we were being pretty silly, but I knew
he was relieved too.

I could hardly wait for the doctor to come, to tell him the
wonderful news. Bless Dr. Hill—perhaps he is too tender-
hearted to be a doctor. When I told him he said: "Good!
That's fine. I hope it's significant."

I couldn't possibly wait for Fred to get back to Perry to
announce the good tidings. I rushed to the telephone and
called Ruth Rogers. The end of the anxiety had come. The
thousands of prayers had been answered. At last she could
announce that Hentz could move!

Later, Charles and I were sitting on a long bench outside the little snack bar. I wanted to be there to see *everybody* and tell the wonderful news. The young doctor who'd had to tell us the seriousness of Hentz's condition that first day came by. He sat down to talk to us a while, and I told him of our great happiness.

He looked at me in amazement, and asked: "Hasn't anyone told you? I'm surprised that some doctor didn't tell you that you could expect this. Surely one of your doctors explained about the movement in your son's knees. All quadriplegics start having muscular spasms about this length of time following their injury. He is not moving his legs voluntarily. He is having muscle spasms."

I jumped up and ran outside with Charles right beside me. My heart and my soul were screaming: "No, no, no! It's not so!"

Nearly as awful as hearing that the movement in my son's knees meant nothing was the horrible thing he called Hentz. A quadriplegic! Such an ugly word! It sounded so permanent, so loathsome, as if it applied to a hideous insect. Words, words, words! Why do doctors have to have so many mysterious, ugly words for hurt people?

I cried while Charles fumed. He was furious with the doctor for hurting me, but I knew the doctor hadn't intended the hurt. He thought it was more cruel for me to believe the thing I yearned to believe.

We weathered this disappointment, and it was well, because there were so many, many more waiting for us. I learned not to flinch at the word, and can now speak of my son as a quadriplegic with composure. It doesn't even hurt too much when people more experienced in these matters call him a "quad." My lack of revulsion for the word didn't come until later, when Hentz was taken to the Institute of Physical Medicine and Rehabilitation in New York. Such words are used so casually there that they become commonplace.

One day Mayor Lewis B. Wilson, of Macon, visited Hentz at the hospital. He had heard about Hentz's great determination, and it appealed to him because the same quality had given meaning and zest to his life after doctors had told him that he would be a semi-invalid. He'd suffered from a crippling form of arthritis, and had been triumphant. Even though the arthritis left his back twisted and his neck crooked, it had not managed to dull his sheer joy of living. After being told that his days of usefulness and activity were ended, he learned to fly a plane, secured a pilot's license, and was elected mayor of the city of Macon. He held the office for six years.

He and Hentz liked each other immediately, and his visits were frequent during Hentz's long hospitalization. One day when he came he brought Hentz a silver badge with his name on it making him an honorary Chief of Police. He also gave him a billy stick with his name on it. I felt a tightening in my heart then, as on so many thousands of other occasions, when I realized that Hentz could only look at the billy and the handsome badge. He couldn't hold them and feel the texture and smoothness of the metal and wood. Such hurts could be your undoing if you didn't have faith. The gifts pleased Hentz tremendously, and he had considerable fun in exercising his newly bestowed authority.

We put these trinkets on his dresser beside the lovely silver badge that the superintendent of schools presented to him at graduation time. Each year a member of the senior class is chosen for traits of leadership, scholarship, and citizenship, an honor bestowed by the Daughters of the American Revolution. I had hoped very much that Hentz would win it. When it was given to Hentz he mumbled: "I think Charles ought to have it. Are you sure you aren't doing this just because I've been hurt?" The superintendent assured him that it had been settled long before Hentz was hurt, but Hentz always insisted that Charles ought to have it. Charles and Hentz were both honor graduates, and even though the school here does not have a valedictorian it was common knowledge that Charles was the top man.

We didn't talk about graduation in Hentz's presence. We thought it would hurt him, but he laughed about our silence later. In Perry the music teacher always plays "Pomp and Circumstance" while the serious, black-gowned seniors advanced down the aisle of the church. In one of the albums that had been given to Hentz was a record of "Pomp and Circumstance," and one day Charles put it on the record player by mistake. He fumbled nervously while he took it off. Hentz didn't say anything then, but a long time afterward he told me that he thought it was funny.

We didn't tell him that the junior-senior banquet had been canceled because of the seriousness of his condition. The young people said they couldn't have a good time while Hentz was in such a critical state. They used the money they had raised by selling magazines, peanuts, and cakes at ball games and contests of various sorts to buy drinking fountains for the school.

Had we known fully of Hentz's inner strength, much anguish could have been spared us. He had difficulty sleeping, a major problem during all of his hospitalization. I hit upon the idea of reading to him whenever he was restless. Since

Hentz prefers biographies, I decided to read from Lud-wig's *Napoleon*. I read during the day, and Fred continued the story at night. Napoleon became such a real personality that at times I fancied I could see him posturing and smirking in the corners of the hospital room. Hentz formed a strong affection for him, and I dreaded the time when our little Corsican would have to die again.

I had to be quick to ad lib the passages in the book that I thought would hurt Hentz. If Mr. Ludwig happened to say, "The long, cold winter and heavy snow had a paralyzing effect on the army," I would quickly substitute another word for "paralyzing."

One morning when I arrived at the hospital Fred told me that Hentz felt curiously depressed. After questioning him I learned that he had finished the book during the night. Fred laughed at me when I suggested that Napoleon's death might be the cause of Hentz's depression. Napoleon's rule may have been ruthless to his suffering fellowmen, but— bless him—he carried us over many rough spots!

When it looked as though Hentz's condition was not one of immediate danger, all of us wanted to meet Mr. Leo Williams, the man who had pulled Hentz out of the lake after the dive. We sent word to him that we would be very happy to have him come to the hospital. He lives in a town about 110 miles from Macon.

When he came in the door I thought he resembled a beard-less Santa Claus. He was short and very fat, with a pleasant face. He seemed awed by the sight of Hentz on the strange-looking bed and with a bandage across his forehead. In a few minutes his warmth and good humor were felt by all of us.

As he talked, I was struck again by the fact that everything seemed to be following a pattern. If there were a pattern wouldn't it have to be a good one? There'd be no sense in following a bad one.

Mr. Williams didn't look athletic; in fact, I couldn't imagine him in swimming trunks. Surely Fate had a hand in it. He said he had not been in swimming in twenty years prior to that day! He drives a school bus in the county where he lives, and had brought a busload of children to Houston Lake for a day's outing. The young men who operated the lake had on hand an immense pair of swimming trunks, and nobody had ever worn them because there'd never been anybody at the lake that large. Out of sheer amusement they insisted that Mr. Williams put on the trunks and go into the water. I think they made wagers about it and had a lot of fun with him. Finally he was persuaded.

He was watching Hentz when he made his dive. When too much time elapsed before Hentz surfaced, Mr. Williams could tell that something was wrong. Hentz went down again —I don't know how many times because I've never asked for the details of the accident. I can't bear to think about it. Anyhow, Mr. Williams pulled Hentz out of the water. Hentz was unconscious then because he was nearly drowned.

We couldn't say what was in our hearts to this lovable man. As he talked, I wondered if Hentz was truly glad that Mr. Williams had put on the big swimming trunks.

About six weeks after the accident Dr. Hill sent for the neurosurgeon in Atlanta to come to Macon to perform a laminectomy. The traction had not succeeded in pulling the jammed vertebrae apart, and Dr. Hill was using as much weight as possible. We knew this was a necessary but serious operation. Dr. Hill assured me that it was no more serious than an appendectomy. Although he didn't expect me to believe that, in his wisdom he sensed that I didn't want to know the whole truth.

Hentz's neck was still terribly swollen, and his appearance was very unnatural. The doctors said that getting the vertebrae back in place would reduce the swelling. Few people expected Hentz to live through this operation, and my hopes were at low ebb. Doubts show in the falseness of a nurse's smile and in a pat on the arm. They show in the compressed lips and noncommittal attitudes of the doctors. I felt uneasy all that day.

About two hours before the operation the Van Divieres came—all three of them. How good of them to know how much we would need them! I responded to her certainty that everything would be all right.

There was great excitement before they took Hentz to the operating room. Dr. Hill permitted Charles Bledsoe to get scrubbed and put on an operating-room gown. Our next-door neighbor, and very dear friend, Mayo Davis, who is known as Pete, also went into the operating room after similar preparation. I remember laughing at how silly they looked, and thinking how unflattering the white gown was to Pete's stomach. I suppose the doctors thought they would be needed to help turn Hentz on the Foster bed. They may have feared that lying on his face for several hours would cause his cheeks to break down as had his forehead.

The neurosurgeon entered Hentz's room and looked at him without speaking to any of us. I seemed to miss in him the gentleness he had shown earlier in the Laboratory Technician's office when he told us that Hentz could not recover. The words he spoke that night were the last he spoke to us.

After a while the orderlies came for Hentz, and rolled him away on his Foster bed. Fred and I followed to the elevator. With cruel definiteness the iron doors again clanged shut on the elevator. My only child had gone again to the great white sterile space on the fifth floor.

We could hear the cables rattling as the elevator strained to its destination. We could hear the heavy doors being opened on the fifth floor. My heart felt as heavy and beaten as those scarred doors. I didn't think Hentz would die during the operation, but I was terribly frightened—both by my ignorance *and* by my understanding. Then a huge hand was laid on my shoulder. I looked up into the face of our minister, who pulled his handkerchief out of his pocket and blew his nose quite loudly and thoroughly. He wasn't ashamed to be seen weeping.

He said: "Come on back to Hentz's room. You might as well sit down."

Somebody had tidied the room and put chairs around for us and for our visitors. Because the floor had just been mopped, there was a strong smell of pine oil. Many people had gathered in Hentz's room for the long wait. As the minister asked us to bow our heads while he offered a prayer to the Heavenly Father, I bit my lip to keep from weeping. I have forgotten the exact words he used to ask his favor of God, but I shall never forget the rightness of them; I shall never forget the intimacy between him and God. His sincerity and simplicity were more eloquent than anything I'd ever heard. As he called upon God's goodness to make everything all well with the boy upstairs in the operating room, I felt a certainty that God would hear his supplication.

When the prayer was finished and we raised our heads, there were no dry eyes. All of us knew we had experienced something very beautiful and comforting. There was the customary embarrassment about letting people see your emotions, and everyone started talking at once.

The dietitian came in with trays of coffee, cake, and ice cream. Mrs. Van Diviere remarked upon the hospital's kindness, and I told her of the great consideration the hospital had shown us.

Dr. Taft, in talking of Hentz's case with the dietitian, had impressed on her the necessary part that food would play in any improvement. With the pressure sore on his back robbing him of his body protein, it was imperative that the protein be replaced, if possible, with food. She came to his room every morning to inquire if he could think of anything that would taste good. She would get squab, shrimp, huge steaks, and even hamburgers if he asked for them! She fixed the trays just like a fastidious hostess trying to impress an important guest. Hentz didn't do her efforts justice, but she kept trying. I think her constant care in preparing his food is largely responsible for his survival.

I described Hentz's condition to Mrs. Van Diviere, and she assured me that it was not alarming. She said that I would have to be patient. She knew how long the wait could be. I didn't know then that I would wait years where she had waited months. It was just as well that I didn't.

The hours dragged on, and Hentz was still in the operating room. Pete or Charles would come to the room occasionally to tell us that all was well. We always laughed at their unbecoming garb, and at Charles's air of importance.

The minister told of his love for Buckshot—his name for all the young boys. He then related the story of his first meeting with Hentz. He had just moved to Perry and was sitting on the front porch of the parsonage. An ancient model-A Ford rattled to a halt in front of the house, and a fine-looking boy got out and walked to the steps. His shoulders were broad, and his hair was fair, and he was tanned the color of new leather. Hentz introduced himself, saying: "Preacher, I'm Hentz Houser. I'm at camp now—going back right this minute. I just wanted you to know that you'll be seeing a lot of me when camp is over. I'm a regular customer at church." He waved gaily and climbed back into his model-A to return to Scout camp where he was a member of the staff.

At last the waiting was over: Hentz was being returned from the operating room. Our group went into the hall to wait. With relief and thankfulness I saw that Hentz was awake. His head and the upper part of his body were in a cast, and the ugly tongs had been removed from his skull. He smiled at me as he passed me in the hall, and I touched him very gently for just a fleeting second. As I do for every big kindness, and every little kindness too, I breathed, "Thank You, God."

The details of that operation are confused in my mind, because there were so many conflicting reports. One of our nurses explained to me that they didn't go into the spinal cord, but that the neurosurgeon made a little opening to see if there would be any discharge of blood, which would indicate the cord had been cut. She assured me that there was no blood, and that that was a very good sign. I did not question any of the doctors. Dr. Hill said that they didn't look at the spinal cord because it would have prolonged the operation, and that Hentz was in no condition for them to have done so in order to satisfy their curiosity.

Charles Van Diviere was at the operating-room door when the surgeon from Atlanta came out. This man was associated with the neurosurgeon who had told the Van Divieres that Charles would have to be in bed all his life because his spinal cord had been severed. I think Charles might have said something about that to the doctor. I do know that he asked him specifically if Hentz's spinal cord was severed, and the surgeon said that it was not. I don't know how he knew if they didn't look. The Atlanta doctor got in his car and departed without saying anything to us, leaving the suturing of the wound to Dr. Hill. Despite the conflicting reports, I felt encouraged. At least they didn't tell us definitely that the cord was severed, and there was reason to hope that it was only bruised. Not often, but in rare cases, there have been recoveries from a bruised cord. I slept better that night, and I was not as tense as usual when I reached the hospital to relieve Fred.

The lessening of tension didn't last, however. I was standing in the hall near my little cot as a doctor came out of a room down the hall. He walked toward me and inquired about Hentz's condition, although he was not one of Hentz's doctors. I didn't think he knew about the operation, and I said, "He had a laminectomy yesterday, and is resting pretty well."

He rubbed his chin with his hand, and said gravely: "Yes, I heard about the operation. It is tragic, so very tragic. You have my deep sympathy. But I suppose that where there's life there is always hope. Anyway, I hope so." He walked away leaving me frightened and confused.

What could he mean except that the outlook was blacker than we had believed? Hentz's spinal cord must be severed, I thought. What was there about the operation that made the situation more tragic?

CHAPTER FIVE

A few days after Hentz's operation I had an experience that I hesitate to tell, because I would not believe it if someone else wrote of it as his experience. I don't want to make anyone skeptical of the authenticity of any part of the story, and I couldn't bear to have anyone laugh about it. I don't pretend to understand it. I know it could be coincidence, but I am inclined to discount that possibility. I tell it because it rescued me from despair so many times that it has a definite place in the story.

I was alone in the room with Hentz. He had been given a sedative, and the nurse had gone to lunch. I tried to read something Mrs. Van Diviere had sent that had helped her. I kept looking at Hentz, lying so still—terribly still! The awful possibility that he would never move again, never put his arms around me and say some boyish nonsense; the thought that I'd never again hear him madly rushing down a flight of stairs—these were almost more than I could bear. I had prayed terribly hard; yet in spite of my prayers, and the thousands of prayers that were being said for him, I knew that every practical person felt hopeless about my son.

Suddenly I remembered something I'd heard recently in

a sermon: We are not bold enough with God! He wants us to approach Him with courage and make our requests known to Him, things our timidity might have held back.

I looked at Hentz's feet. The weather was warm and he was uncovered. They were resting against a board, with pillows between the soles and the board to prevent pressure sores. Mrs. Van Diviere had told us never to let his feet drop; to do so would cause dropped ankles; and, when he was learning to walk again, surgery might be required to correct it. Hentz's feet were so still, everything in the room was so still, that nothing seemed real. As I watched Hentz's feet I thought of something Fred had said a day or two before: "I'd give a million dollars if one of Hentz's toes would move." One of the doctors had told us that if there was any return of muscular function or feeling it would probably be in the feet first, because the nerves controlling the feet were deeper in the spinal cord and the healing process would affect them first.

Suddenly the anxiety and waiting and suspense swept over me in great waves. I must know! I simply must! I couldn't go on and on every day looking for something that didn't happen. If someone only knew!

Then the boldness the minister had spoken of took hold of me. In the old days people asked God for signs! I would ask for some kind of sign. I prayed. I said all the things I had been taught that form a prayer, such as, "If it be Thy will," but I went much further than that. What kind of sign could I ask God for? All at once I knew! I prayed again: "If my prayer can be heard and answered, and if my son will be well, please, God, let the toe on his right foot move. Then, God, I shall take that as a promise from You that our son will be healed. Amen."

I raised my head slowly and fixed my attention on his right foot. I watched so intently that concentration made me dizzy. Every now and then I whispered, "Oh, *please!*" I think if the building had caught fire at that moment I would not have moved or taken my eyes off Hentz's foot.

And then I saw it! Slowly, ever so slowly, the large toe came forward! Then it moved back again. It did it again and again. When I was able to move, I walked to the window to look out, thinking my senses must have betrayed me. When my head felt clear, and the light-filled specks were no longer dancing madly before my eyes, I returned to my chair by the bed. I looked again. There was no denying it: the toes were moving! I had the terrible feeling that I was actually in the presence of God, and I felt unworthy to be there. I could hardly believe that such a thing had happened to me—that I had such a power—to have God do this thing because I had asked Him.

The nurse came in, but I said nothing to her about the toes moving. After a while she saw it, and cried out so loudly that she awakened Hentz. He saw it. When Fred came that night, he saw it. Many other people saw it too—but none knew what it meant to me.

Now it can be explained. Muscular spasms might have caused his knees to move; but the strange thing is that the knees kept moving, and do to this day, but the toes don't. I can't remember them moving any more since that day, and possibly a day or so following it. But why should such movement begin at the moment I prayed? Whenever I was filled with doubt, I would say, "It was just caused by muscle spasms." Then the thought would occur to me: Suppose it was only muscle spasms. Do you think God would let such a cruel coincidence happen at that very moment? I believe that God has a hand in all matters, great and small: I believe that He gave me the sign I prayed for.

I don't think about this incident very often now; perhaps I should. It is one more of the deep mysteries that happened that I cannot explain.

The only times I saw Fred were for a few minutes at the hospital in the morning and briefly at night. On some days he would leave before Charles Bledsoe and I arrived. I always looked far ahead as I drove to Macon, hoping to see Leonora's light green car coming toward us. I knew then that Hentz was not worse, or Fred would have remained. It was good to stop a minute on the busy highway and talk to him. Fred was always cheerful; I don't think I ever heard him say he'd had a bad night, although some of them must have been hideous. I always held my head a little higher when he whispered, from his car to mine, "I'm proud of you." He meant he was proud that I could carry my part of the burden without collapsing and leaving him with a still heavier load. He meant, too, that my optimism made it easier for him to meet the trials of his business day. What strength was his, and how his unfailing good cheer helped me!

During the long afternoons Charles Bledsoe and I often glanced at our watches, anxious for the hour to come when Fred and Louise and Leonora would arrive. Everybody loved Fred; the nurses and all the people in the hospital called him Pop, just as Hentz did. When Pop comes, things get better!

Many times I've thought that Fred and I were like actors giving a performance. But did our courage make us give a good performance, or did the performance give us the courage? I've never come to a definite conclusion, but I believe that acting courageous one day ceases to be acting, and when faith is added to it, it becomes courage. I never let down in the little details. I kept my face powdered and lipstick on my lips. Late at night, when I came in from the hospital too weary to breathe, I shampooed my hair. I never knew when someone might come that doubted our courage, and I wanted my appearance to match my actions. I enjoyed the surprised observations of visitors: "How do you manage to look so rested? I expected to find you looking worn out."

There was just the waiting now. There did not seem to be any improvement in Hentz's condition. Every day was like the previous one.

One day during August we told Dr. Hill that we wanted to go to Atlanta so that Hentz might get the physical therapy he needed so terribly. His arms and shoulders were very painful, and so stiffened that nursing care was extremely difficult. There was not a registered therapist in Macon. Because a patient couldn't be admitted to the hospital for the express purpose of getting physical therapy, a doctor had to admit him for other reasons. Dr. Hill and all the other doctors hoped that at the larger hospital in Atlanta something could be done about the ulcer on Hentz's back. Dr. Hill made the arrangements.

The trip to Atlanta from Macon was torturous. A friend of ours who owned the funeral home in Perry offered to take Hentz in his new Cadillac ambulance. He devised some kind of cooling system, hoping to counteract some of the relentless August heat. He also arranged with the State Patrol to escort us on the trip. Hentz's room in Macon had been air-conditioned, and moving him out into the heat was a risk. He cannot perspire because the paralysis prevents him from doing so, and, when Nature's cooling system is impaired, getting overheated is dangerous.

Charles and I followed the ambulance in our car, and barely avoided an accident when a piece of road machinery made a left turn in front of us. We were driving too fast, so as not to lose the ambulance because they would need us when they reached the hospital. We knew how to handle Hentz, and strangers didn't. Though the nurse, who had been on duty in the mornings since the beginning of Hentz's hospitalization, and Fred were in the ambulance they would need Charles and me to help.

When we reached the hospital Hentz was very sick, and had a temperature of 105.

The Macon Hospital permitted our nurse to bring all the necessary charts so that the new nurses and doctors would know what had been done.

Late that first afternoon the doctor who admitted Hentz called us into the hall after his preliminary examination and said: "If I had known the boy's condition I would have advised Dr. Hill not to send him here. He is not in an operable condition; his protein count is much too low." There was discouragement from the beginning. We wanted to tell him that Dr. Hill knew Hentz was not ready for surgery, but he had hoped that in a larger hospital there would be improved facilities for getting him ready.

The first night set a pattern for what was to follow. The supervisor would not permit Fred to stay with Hentz because the hospital was crowded; our son was sharing a room with another patient. Though we could not secure the services of a special nurse, we got a practical nurse to care for Hentz and his roommate.

The first night was one of terror for Hentz. The doctor wrote on the chart that Hentz was to be turned every two hours. His shoulders were so painful from lack of use that turning him had been out of the question except on the orthopedic frame, which did not put pressure on his shoulders. Every two hours a nurse came and turned him—while he begged not to be. He was alone for the first time since he had been hurt, and everything was strange. The nurse became very impatient because Hentz protested so violently at being turned, and she said harsh, cruel things to him. We were distressed to learn, when we reached the hospital, how he had suffered. We determined that neither of us would leave him alone again. We found the superintendent and secured a private room in a new wing of the hospital. A few days later the original nurse was transferred to that floor as night supervisor. At no time during Hentz's illness did he feel as unfriendly toward any person as he did to this nurse. He actually seemed physically afraid of her, and physical fear was something he'd never known. She tried to be kind after she knew more about Hentz's case, but he never regained confidence in her.

The nurse from Macon, who by now was a beloved friend, left on the second day. I had a sinking feeling as I watched her walk down the marble hall, leaving us alone to begin another adjustment in a strange hospital.

A few minutes after the nurse left I entered an elevator to go in search of a telephone, and was overjoyed to see a friend who had been through an ordeal similar to ours. Mattilu Hodge's husband, Warren, had suffered a cerebral thrombosis the day before Hentz was hurt. He was also a patient in the Macon Hospital. Warren was forty-three when he was stricken, and his condition was as desperate as Hentz's.

Warren and Hentz were from the same county, and their illness was the cause of much concern. The county paper carried large black headlines announcing the two tragedies.

Warren, who was a very successful businessman in a town ten miles from Perry, was full of the joy of living and giving, and would do anything to perfect one of his complicated practical jokes. Some were not so practical, however, because he would spare no expense to see one well carried out. Though he played too hard and worked too hard, he derived great satisfaction from seeing his efforts accomplish so much. Even though the doctor told him that his blood pressure was very high, Warren paid no heed. One day, while he was presiding at a meeting of the Cotton Ginners' Association in Macon, he was stricken. He was in a coma for three weeks, and there was little hope that he would live. Mattilu never gave up, however, and she was supported in her faith by Dr. Taft and her brother who was intern in the Macon Hospital. He wouldn't give up, either. How they fought for Warren! At the end of three weeks he opened his eyes; and as soon as he did *he* started fighting too! He was almost completely paralyzed, and his eyes were fixed in a stare ahead of him. I know now that when there is joy in a person, *nothing* can kill it. Though Warren's laugh sounded guttural and unnatural because of the tracheotomy, he could still laugh!

The paralysis lessened, and Warren began using one hand and arm. He couldn't walk, but his general condition improved steadily. When he heard that Hentz had gone to Atlanta in the hopes of getting physical therapy, he decided that that was what he needed too. They arrived a day after we did.

How good to see Mattilu! How many nights we had sat side by side in a darkened spot in the hospital, virtually holding our breaths in fear of what the next minute might bring! How many times did we remind each other of the comforting twelve words: *All things work together for good for those who love the Lord!* As I looked at her in the elevator, I marveled at her cool, unruffled beauty. She looked like something out of *Vogue.* Who would think she'd ever had a care in the world? I've never seen her really cry. Sometimes tears would roll down her cheeks, but she allowed herself no more than that.

Because Fred and Warren had both attended the university that is connected with the hospital, Mattilu and I had the privilege of rooming in the beautiful alumni building, near the hospital. Charles stayed in Hentz's room at night, and I stayed with Mattilu. She was good for me because of her tranquillity.

The doctors had not said what they thought about Hentz's condition. I think one of them planned to tell me one day, but I stopped him. He knocked on the door and I stepped into the hall. I was disturbed by the grave expression on his face. When he began to speak I said: "Please don't give me bad news today. I don't want to hear it." I wanted to say that perhaps I could hear it with more calmness when Fred came for a visit, but not alone. He must have understood, because nothing was said until Fred came.

One day Fred, Charles, and I were in Hentz's room talking. One of the doctors entered and said a few routine things. When he neared the door he motioned to Fred and me to follow him. By now I knew that when the doctors motioned for you to go into the hall it meant more heartbreak. Without stopping outside Hentz's door, the doctor continued down the hall and into an unoccupied room.

The room was very orderly, as if somebody had just died,

our endurance. And maybe it *was* God's will for Hentz to live. It was with no feeling of rebelliousness or defiance to God's plans that we resolved to fight. Through all our trials I never felt that I was fighting God's will in anything, but helping Him by fulfilling an obligation.

Discouragement. Defeat. Gloom. Despair. We had thought things would be better now, but at every turn one disappointment followed the other. Wearily I repaired my face with makeup. I returned to Hentz's room and pretended that nothing had happened. Of course, Charles was not fooled. He knew that we were faced with another crisis.

We hope that someone else faced with such a choice will have the courage to fight on and on and on. A doctor later told us that if Hentz had been given the alcohol block he might never have regained the use of his arms. There is a probability that it would have made them insensitive for so many years that the arm muscles might have atrophied. Hentz could not have lived at home, because we could not have treated the urinary infections which constantly plagued him.

As I dragged wearily toward my room late that night, I felt dizzy, and I had the familiar sensation of being violently whirled downward. I wondered if I had the strength to climb out of my black despair. Perhaps it would be easier, after all, to give up; but I discarded that thought immediately. I would never give up! I had to plan my fight more carefully. I could still hear the doctor saying, "There is nothing medical science can do for your son." Well, the help would have to come from elsewhere.

A bath helped a little, and telling Mattilu helped greatly. As I got into bed, I had the Bible under my arm. It was one of the graduation gifts I had bought for Hentz, and had given to him a day or two before the accident. This Bible was dearer to me than any others we owned. The exquisitely fine leather felt good to the touch, but that wasn't all. I had thought that Hentz would keep it all his life, and tell his children that his mother gave it to him when he finished high school. I had hoped it would bring him wisdom and understanding as he lived his abundant life. Now he couldn't even hold it in his hands, or turn its pages.

I turned to the New Testament because only the books that told of Jesus' stay on earth were able to comfort me. I read and reread the accounts of the miracles. Perhaps there was a secret there that I would find if I kept looking. The miracle that I liked best was Christ's healing of the blind (Matthew 9:27-30). When Jesus said, "Believe ye that I am able to do this?" the blind man answered, "Yea, Lord." It sounded so simple. All he had to do was to believe. And Jesus said to him, "According to your faith be it unto you." According to your faith be it done. That night I prayed for faith, and more faith. I did not pray for Hentz that night. If my son's recovery depended on faith, then I had a grave responsibility. I asked God to let me turn a deaf ear to all discouragements, and believe that He would spare Hentz. I didn't sleep until the morning hours, but when I did it was with a feeling of inner calm that I hadn't known in a long time.

I went to the hospital very early and peered into Hentz's room. He and Charles were still asleep. Charles still had on his clothes, but he looked comfortable on the little cot. I walked out to sit on the long terrace that connected the wings of the huge hospital. After a while a nurse rolled a young woman patient out in a wheel chair and left her to enjoy the early-morning coolness. I smiled and nodded a good morning to her. She wanted to talk, and rolled her chair close to mine.

In a sort of excited, breathless way she said, "I just saw that boy up the hall."

I thought I knew which boy she meant, but I hoped she didn't mean Hentz. I asked, "Which boy?"

"The one on the funny bed. You know, the one who broke his neck. He was just lying there so still. They say he can't move at all. The nurses say he is wonderful—just laughs and jokes all the time. They say he can't live much longer."

In an instant this strange, jabbering little woman had destroyed all the composure I had prayed so hard to possess. She didn't know, of course, that I was the boy's mother, and I didn't tell her. I tried to smile at her while my heart was choking me. Could she hear its tortured thumping? So that was what the nurses were telling the other patients! God, let us show all of them!

That night, after I went to bed, I fought the battle over again. Somehow I came through still determined to go on with the fight—and to fight harder than ever. The next morning one of the doctors saw me in the reception room and stopped to talk. He said: "We wish there were some encouragement we could give you. We think for your good that you should be made to realize that nothing can be done. It must sound heartless to you, but we feel very deeply for you and wish we could help you. It would be better for you, and better for your son, if he were at home."

Proudly, and even defiantly, I answered him. He was a kind man, and had been very gentle and considerate of Hentz. I meant no reflection on what they had done when I said: "We won't take him home. If you can't help him, we shall continue to look, and keep looking, until we find someone who thinks they can. We are *not* giving up!"

Physical therapists must be the world's most consistent optimists. Dr. Robert Bennett, who is the Medical Director of the Foundation at Warm Springs is the chairman of the Department of Physical Medicine at the Atlanta hospital. After consultation with Hentz's doctors, he decided to try some of the exercises and other therapy. Hentz had never been in a sitting position, and we could not transfer him from his bed to a stretcher because of his painful shoulders, so we rolled him to the Physical Medicine Department in his bed. His fever was very high, but so were his hopes. Because the therapist assigned to Hentz was busy with another patient when we arrived, Hentz had to wait a while. As he was lying there, a very beautiful girl of sixteen or seventeen rolled her wheel chair close to his bed. She asked him why he was there, and if he'd had polio. She'd had polio two years previously, and had not walked since.

When she left, Hentz said to me: "Well, I suppose I have something to be thankful for. I'm glad I didn't have polio. I feel so sorry for that girl." He didn't know that his injury was more serious than polio. I had to walk away, and around a corner, where he could not see the tears that I couldn't hold back. One of the therapists saw me standing there and came over and put her arms around my shoulders.

"Don't cry. Your son will be all right. You just wait and see!" After so many long months of gloom, somebody had said a few encouraging words! I didn't think I'd ever heard anything so beautiful. I soon found out that that was the attitude of the entire department.

The therapist assigned to Hentz had a powerful personality. I saw a light of interest and approval in Hentz's eyes as she began talking. She was directly under the doctor from Warm Springs, and we were very fortunate to get her. As she worked on Hentz she explained everything she did. When she moved one of his legs she'd say: "You must keep these muscles in good condition so that when he ties his shoes there won't be any tightness. You must exercise his ankles so that when he walks there won't be any stiffness." *When* he walks! She massaged the tight shoulders until the tears came into his eyes, but he tightened his jaws and bore it. She found muscles in his arms—muscles that could not be used because of his sore shoulders. She told him the names of the muscles and what their functions were. She was radiant with cheer and hope. She'd heard about the unhappy prognosis the doctors had given us, and encouraged us to keep on hoping in spite of it. "They are good doctors," she said, "but I've seen too many people do things that doctors said they couldn't do. Something besides science enters in, in rare cases." I knew what she meant. Most of all we loved her for saying "when" instead of "if."

She was horrified when she saw the ulcer on Hentz's back, and said it was the worst one she had ever seen. She told Charles, Felton, and me what to do. She made me do things I had never done before; but it never occurred to me not to obey her. She insisted that Hentz eat, whether he liked his food or not, because without protein his ulcer would not heal. Her attitude was so positive that she left us stimulated and exhilarated.

One day she failed to appear. The hours went by slowly as we waited for her visit to the room. Nor did she come the next day. I went to the desk to find out why. The nurses there probably knew, but they called the Physical Medicine

Department to inquire. I could hear her talking, and indignantly she told the nurse that she had been instructed by the doctors not to work with Hentz any more. She said they thought it was useless. Useless! When she now could move Hentz's arms up, backward and forward! He could move his shoulders because her strong fingers had worked out the stiffness. But most of all she had been such a boost to his morale. I felt stunned and beaten.

Our next-door neighbor, Pete Davis, and his wife were visiting at the hospital at the time. Pete was the mayor of Perry, and also a state senator. He is the kind of person who knows how to get things done, and he was indignant. He has a lot of charm, and he can be very persuasive. I was glad they were there, because I knew that if anyone could help us Pete could. I didn't see how I could go back to Hentz's room and tell him that the therapist could not work with him any more. He would have grasped the meaning. Our good friend went to the telephone. He called the doctor at Warm Springs; he called Fred; he called on the superintendent of the hospital; he talked to some of our doctors. Before he was through we were assured that the therapist would be back with Hentz the very next day.

We learned much from that exuberant therapist that is helpful even yet. From her we learned how to prevent any more pressure sores from developing, and how to care for the existing ones.

Hentz and Charles still laugh about the rough time we had in Atlanta. Hentz said it was the first time the full impact of the extent of his injury had hit him. In Macon he had been so protected in every way that any small detail that might hurt him was avoided. He had so much company there that he didn't have much time to think.

When the Atlanta doctors realized that we had no intention of taking Hentz home, they suggested that we take him back to Macon to be under the care of Dr. Hill. By this time we suspected that they didn't want Hentz in the Atlanta hospital and thought it a waste of time and effort to treat him. We called Dr. Hill and asked if we could bring Hentz back to the Macon Hospital, and when he said we could we made arrangements with a young man to treat Hentz twice a week. He was in charge of the Physical Medicine Department in a nearby veterans' hospital, and had heard about Hentz. He called Fred and offered his services twice each week. We felt relieved and thankful for that much, although Hentz needed the therapy daily.

On the day we were to leave Atlanta, I was called into the reception room to see guests. I recognized, and spoke to, Margery Short from Perry, although I had never known her intimately. She was with some other people, and I don't remember everything that was said. I know only that the outcome of that visit was one of the best things that ever happened to us.

Margery said she was on her way back to Perry from Nashville, Tennessee. She had just finished work on her Master's degree. She had been a missionary for two years and had several months' leave before going back to the field. At one time she was in Warsaw, but the Communists made her leave, and from there she went to North Africa. I think she said she had to return in October. During the war she was a WAC and worked in hospitals behind the front lines doing physical therapy. She wanted to know if she could work with Hentz until she went back to Africa. I could hardly believe my ears. The young man who had offered to help would be relieved because we knew he couldn't really

spare the time to drive to Macon from his hospital to treat
Hentz. Then, too, Margery would be there every day. The
doctors in Macon would have to agree to the arrangement,
but I knew they would. She was quiet and efficient-looking. I
had heard wonderful reports about her, and I knew our
church was proud to have sent her into the mission field. I
knew she was intellectual and capable, but there was much
about her that I did not know. At that moment I felt that
she was sent from Heaven. *Now* I *know* she was sent from
Heaven. Her offer made the defeat of the Atlanta experience
less bitter.

When we got back to Macon we found that the people at
the hospital had assigned Hentz to his old room, and had
had it freshly painted. It was so good to return to the place
we had left with hopes soaring high!

CHAPTER SIX

Margery was small, blond, and quiet, with twinkling eyes. She is one of the most unselfish people I've ever known. I don't suppose she has ever considered her comfort, wants, or pleasure in all of her life. She is the perfect example of Christianity with a sense of humor. She could be quite stubborn at times, and whenever she took a stand she was unmovable. She was fun to be with, and the sheer joy of living and sharing made her radiant. A cousin of mine, Janie Smith Rhyne, had a poem in her book *Salt Wind* that describes Margery: she is "glad of life and sure of God."

The morning after Hentz's return to the Macon Hospital, I drove by to get Margery to bring her to the hospital with Charles and me. She came out her front door skipping, and she skipped out every morning to follow, except on the days when our hearts were exceptionally heavy because of the suffering Hentz was having to bear. She disliked shoes, and wore the things that were the least like them that she could find.

As soon as Margery arrived at the hospital she would put the chemically filled packs on Hentz's shoulders. Then, when the heat had loosened the tight muscles, she would gently massage his arms, shoulders, and legs. She was very gentle, and I saw Hentz's relief when he knew that she would not hurt him. From the first day it was obvious that she would never consciously do anything to hurt or to displease him. She was completely under his spell. I think he had been a little worried about her being a missionary, because his impressions of those good souls came largely from the movies. He soon discovered that her calling in life would never make him feel cramped. Though her goodness is recognized by everyone, it is the kind that allows other people to retain their naturalness. She, Charles, Hentz, and I spent every day together until Charles entered college in late September. Then there were three of us.

One of our most faithful visitors was a young Catholic priest. I don't suppose Hentz had ever known a Catholic, much less a priest, but we looked forward to his twice-a-day visits. He was a very happy person, and enjoyed the easy manner in which we welcomed him. We were not disrespectful, but we did tease him a lot. He was quite a talker, and told us often that he wanted to enter a monastery. Of course, we always laughed, because we couldn't imagine him obeying the rule of silence. He and Margery used to argue over the merits of becoming a martyr—a condition that did not appeal to Margery at all, but that somehow appealed to the priest. After Margery had returned to Africa, he told me that she was the most saintly person he'd ever known.

One night the priest invited Margery to address a group of young adults at his church. She agreed, and both of us drove to the parish, where we parked the car in the rear of the church. We were pleased to find such ample parking space. Margery made a splendid talk on the status of women in Africa. When she finished talking, and the meeting adjourned, we went to the car to drive the twenty-eight miles home to Perry. We discovered that our car was surrounded by dozens of other cars, making it impossible to get out. The priest saw our predicament and said he would ask the people to move their cars. In another part of the church the weekly bingo game was well under way. The people began filing out to move their cars. There was such a disturbance and delay that the players decided to go home. We had broken up the bingo game! I told Margery it would make a good story: "Methodist missionary breaks up bingo game." Everything was fun with Margery.

The priest was not always lighthearted. On the days that Hentz's suffering was intense the priest was sympathetic, and the words of comfort he whispered helped Hentz very much. One day he told me that I had made a great contribution to the world. I wondered just what he meant. He explained that having a son like Hentz was a great help to the poor old world. Though I was pleased, I didn't feel that I was responsible for that contribution. Then one day Hentz's pain was so excruciating that none of us thought we could bear it much longer; nothing seemed to bring relief. The young priest whispered to Hentz: "The world is made better by your suffering. Please don't think it is a senseless thing. The world is benefiting by it. Christ had to suffer too." Somehow this assurance helped Hentz more than anything we had been able to say. If the world was truly being made richer, Hentz decided to try to bear it graciously.

Shortly after Margery started working with Hentz, Fred and I discussed what we would do about paying her. It was a delicate question, and one he left to me. One day, while riding to Macon, I decided to broach the matter. I told

Margery that we wanted to pay her what other therapists made, or what any private nurse made. Surely no therapist could ever spend as much time with a patient as Margery spent with Hentz. She was visibly embarrassed. "No. I don't want money. I'm thankful that I am able to do this. I feel deeply grateful for the privilege of working with a person like Hentz. I learned one thing during the war. Out of all that suffering I learned something that now is my philosophy of life. I believe with all my heart that every human being is responsible for every other human being on earth."

She said it so simply and sincerely that I knew that all she said was the truth. Giving brings happiness to her; and if I had any doubts the expression on her face when she greeted my son a few minutes later would have dissolved them. Seeing Hentz respond to her tender care was reward enough for her.

Hentz and Margery whispered and laughed a lot, and I wouldn't give them the satisfaction of voicing my curiosity. One day, as I returned from the kitchen with the beautiful tray the dietitian prepared every day for Hentz, I saw that they were excited and delighted over something.

"Look, Mother! Look!" Hentz was slowly lifting his left wrist. Margery had done that. She'd found the weak wrist muscle and worked with it until Hentz now could lift his hand! They would not tell me until the little muscle was strong enough to do its work. So that was what the whispered conferences were about! Lifting a wrist slowly may not sound important to people who lift their hands at will, but to us it was a miracle. Now he could move both arms and a wrist! Margery said this gave us reason to hope for the return of the use of other muscles. Later she found the *pectoralis major*

—one of the important chest muscles. That one was to us like a brave warrior because of its name. We always called that muscle "he" instead of "it." Then, still later, Margery found the other wrist muscle. There may have been gratitude pictured on other faces at the end of a long weary search for a heart's desire, but nothing I've ever witnessed can compare with the pure joy on her face when she had found a new muscle. God was very good indeed to send us Margery.

We were constantly amazed at Hentz's witticisms. If there was a particle of humor in any situation, he saw it. It kept all of us keyed up and at our best so that we could be equally witty on occasion. Woe unto one of us who made any statement without carefully weighing it beforehand! Oh, there were silly things like putting the little turtle, with the grim and uncompromising expression on his face, named Mr. Westmore, for the supervisor of the orderlies, between two slices of bread and wrapping him carefully and sending him to a student nurse who was sick in a room across the hall. She was blessed with a sense of humor too, because she sent it back with a huge half-circle out of the bread as if she'd bitten it. Then one day the lady in the adjoining room was entertaining a roomful of Methodist preachers who were in Macon attending a conference. Hentz had a precious little walking elephant a friend of mine had sent, and we wound him up and let him nonchalantly walk right into the very proper gathering.

I think that sometimes our laughter shocked people who wondered how we could laugh in the face of our tragedy. During the first days following Hentz's accident I didn't think I could ever laugh again—but I'm so thankful I can! Hentz is glad we laughed; years later he said it was the thing that made the difference between making it and not making it.

Being able to laugh is one of the best rewards of an implicit belief that *All things work together for good for those who love the Lord.*

One day while Hentz was still on the orthopedic bed, and unable to see anyone in the room unless the person was quite close to the head of the bed, a woman came down our hall selling fancy handmade articles. It was obvious that she had been a beautiful woman in her youth, and she was still handsome in a mature way. She knocked on the door, and I stepped outside to see what she wanted. She told me she used to sing professionally, and named some important engagements. She said she had heard about my son, and wondered if she could sing for him. She said it would give her pleasure. I couldn't find an excuse, and therefore gave my consent.

Hentz was listening to Arthur Godfrey, and I knew if she had been Patrice Munsel herself she couldn't compete with Godfrey. He was very firm about interruptions during this broadcast. I opened the door and told him that a "nice lady" wanted to sing for him. Charles stepped over to turn the radio off. Margery, Charles, and I stood at respectful attention. Then she began. I think we all jumped under the impact of so much sound in the small room. The song was "Oh, Promise Me," and she gave it everything she had! What she had lost in tone control was compensated for by volume. The windows fairly rattled. Hentz couldn't see her because she was standing at the foot of the bed. He muttered, out of the side of his mouth, "Great balls of fire, who loused up the music?" Charles and I at one side of the bed, and Margery on the other were bursting! I sneaked a look at Margery, but I knew I'd better not try that again if we were to get through the impromptu concert with any dignity. Charles kept tapping my foot with his, and I tried to cut my eyes around to him with a warning. During the solemn rendition nurses and supervisors came dashing down the hall to peep in our door to see if we were all right. The noise had permeated every corner of the old hospital. She sang on unperturbed, and I know she never appeared before a sillier audience.

We had another concert that affected me differently. The colored help in the kitchen knew Hentz because he had been in the hospital for such a long time, and they had tried in every way they knew to prepare foods that would tempt his poor appetite. They were all interested because they'd read and heard about the young boy who was fighting and laughing. The maid and the dishwashers knew him. One day the head cook told me that they wanted to come to Hentz's room and sing some spirituals. When they finished their work that day, they filed in. There were twelve of them—tall ones, thin ones, short ones, and stout ones—all tired from a hard day's work.

Then they began to sing. Though all Negro spiritual singers begin with "Swing Low, Sweet Chariot," it has never grown commonplace by repetition. They sang several of the more familiar spirituals. The untrained voices mingled in perfect harmony as they sang plaintively about their trials and troubles, and Jesus' love for them. The closing song was "Were You There When They Crucified My Lord?"

I turned to the window, and when they left I could not thank them because I couldn't speak. The beauty of their singing and the beauty of their desire to do something pleasing for Hentz brought a lump in my throat.

On our rides to Macon, Margery and I did our serious talking. I don't recall that she ever discussed her particular beliefs, but she did say that she probably wasn't very orthodox. Surely her good deeds speak with a ringing clarity that outdoes mere words. She told me that she'd been so hurt by the cruelty of the war that for a year afterward she could not pray at all. During the war she saw sincerely Christian men die despite their prayers for protection. She had prayed with them, and still they died. Though she didn't understand it then, later she resolved her dilemma. Thereafter she committed herself to becoming a missionary.

On one occasion her mother told me that Margery left Poland with no more than the clothes she had on her back. When I asked her about it she shrugged and said, "It would have been very absurd for me to bring trunks filled with clothes out of Poland." Out of the little pittance she made, she was educating two young people.

Margery was scheduled to return to her work in October, but she asked for an extension. Nothing we could say would shake her determination to stay with us until our plans for a future course of action were settled. All of us had one dream, one goal, and that was to get Hentz to New York to the Institute of Physical Medicine and Rehabilitation. Margery quietly stated that she would stay until Hentz could go to New York.

Though by now Hentz was eating a little better, and scar tissue was beginning to form around the edges of the ulcer on his back, at best it would take a year for it to close. Surgery seemed the only answer, but the doctors said he was not ready. His hospitalization in Macon dragged on and on.

Margery got extension after extension to stay with the boy who needed her so much.

After we came back from Atlanta we had only one special nurse, the one that had been with Hentz from the beginning. Hentz was devoted to her. She knew when to be tender with him, and when to be firm. She was wonderfully sympathetic when his suffering was great, and there was perfect understanding between them. She shared our love and respect for Margery.

There was always company to help pass the long hours. Friends continued to come even as the weeks stretched into long months. I'll never forget the friend who came every other day with appetizing foods, always hoping to bring the thing that would tempt Hentz to eat. She must have made a carload of meringue kisses filled with pecans because she knew they were a source of protein. She was a busy woman who was writing a book, and I often wondered how she could afford to give us so much of her time.

My very dear friend Anne Griffin taught at Wesleyan College in Macon, and it was so good to have her stop by the hospital on her way home from school. I don't think I was nearly as brave as Anne thought I was, but I kept trying to be so that I wouldn't disappoint her. She had so many gifts, and so much to give. She gave so much love and understanding, and was inspiring and could express herself in the most beautiful way. She could make me believe in myself; and the more I believed in myself, the more I believed in God. It was wonderful to let her talk me into riding home with her to have supper and to talk about matters worlds removed from hospitals. How our spirits lifted when we saw her at the hospital door loaded down with lobster salad, hot rye bread covered with garlic butter, and coffee! She worried because Fred and I had to eat at the little snack bar in the hospital.

So many people have wondered how I could bear those long months at the hospital; but they were not really tiresome. Except for the anxiety, they were interesting. We were seldom alone, and we met such wonderful people.

There were days of heartbreak, of course, that were difficult to endure. Those were the days when Hentz suffered so unbearably. The doctors did everything imaginable to relieve his pain, but nothing really helped. They inserted procaine in his veins, and different spinal injections, but the pain continued relentlessly. Later, a neurosurgeon in New York told me that they'd never been able to explain the pain that some quadriplegics suffer. During these periods the laughter and gaiety were gone; everything was crowded out but the pain. Sometimes Hentz would look at me and ask me why. Why? I didn't know what kind of answer to give him, though I yearned to say something that would make the situation sound sensible to him. All I could say was: "Some day we'll know. Of that I am certain." Nor did Margery try to tell him why, though her heart was crying out for the answer. Her touch, and the understanding in her eyes, spoke for her. The pain occurred in the lower part of Hentz's back, and lasted for days at a time; then it would disappear for a while, only to return again. Time and repetition do not dull a mother's sensitivity to her child's suffering. Yet all I could do was to stand by his bed and fight back the feeling of futility and helplessness.

At such times I yearned for the solitude in prayer that, after such trying days, brought me closer to God because there was nothing *we* could do to help. I relied upon the thought that when I was alone in the house in Perry I could cry out to God to be merciful to us and that I would finally find a measure of peace. I knew that then I would sleep and wake again feeling revived and strengthened anew for whatever the day had in store.

I don't know what my husband's visions are, or what his conception of God is—people usually keep these things in the depths of their hearts. I do know that his faith has kept his joy of living a beautiful, vibrant thing. I know that I never felt that I was in touch with God unless I could see His face in my mind's eye. Until I had that vision before me, my mind wandered and I did not feel that I was close to God.

To make Him more real to me during those trying days, I liked to picture Him in a setting which is very dear to me. Jesus loved the sea, and I love the sea, and it seemed a right and fitting place for us to meet. I was most at peace when I visualized Jesus walking by the water's edge with me beside Him. Sometimes we would stop and rest in the shade of an old fishing wharf. In that vision I don't remember that I ever spoke to Him, but He knew what was in my heart. Though He took my hand, I could never look into His face. As we gazed out upon the water, not speaking, my heart cried out for His mercy in restoring my son to health and activity.

Then Jesus would say, very softly, "Look, my child."

I would look up the beach to see Hentz running toward us with his head held high. His body was bronzed from the sun, and he had on the green swimming trunks he wore when he was hurt. He was laughing as he splashed along the water's edge on flying feet. Tricks of the mind? Self-hypnosis? No, I don't think so. Self-deception couldn't bring quiet to a heart as heavy and burdened as mine.

We all need a vision to strive toward and to hold on to. That is my vision, and it brings me hope and comfort. The cynics can laugh; but if, on the day I died, I were to discover that it was all a mistake I would still be glad that I had believed.

CHAPTER SEVEN

The long waiting began to make New York take on the maddening aspects of a mirage. We kept saying: "Keep your chin up, Hentz. When we get to New York you will be helped." I knew he must wonder, along with me: "When? When? When?" What could we tell him? He couldn't be admitted at the Institute of Rehabilitation until the ulcer on his back was closed. Could all of us hold out for another year? Could Fred spend 365 nights on the roll-away bed beside his son in the little room? Could I think of enough cheering things to say to keep my son's morale from flagging? Could I go through another year of coming home from the hospital at 10:00 or 11:00 P.M. and sleeping in the house alone—not afraid of anything that crept or crawled or prowled, but sometimes so afraid of the future? Waiting takes so much out of one.

Hentz's doctors said his protein count had to be increased before they could do anything about the pressure sore. Dr. Taft talked him into swallowing all kinds of concoctions that contained the precious protein. I knew Hentz must hate the word; we spoke so much about it. There is no easy way to get protein: it was administered either by an infusion or by

75

mouth. The mixtures were awful, but Hentz said he would swallow anything if he didn't have to take it intravenously.

Hentz wasn't always sweet. I remember a time when the dietitian came into Hentz's room with a foaming, frothy glass. She told him it was a delicious mixture of chocolate milk and ice cream, but she whispered to me that she'd slipped in two raw eggs and some powdered protein. Hentz had become as cagey as a mouse eyeing a bit of cheese in a trap. She coaxed and begged him to drink it, but he refused. She tried various kinds of persuasion but without success. Finally she said, "Well, you might as well drink it because I'm going to stay right here until you do!"

Wearily he said, "In that case you'd better ring for an orderly to bring you a bed, because you're going to be here for a long time."

Dr. Hill began to notice a change in Hentz. I told him that I was worried because Hentz didn't want company and because he begged to be alone. Being a wise man, he knew it was time for some kind of change. Friends had helped Hentz over so many bad places that now it frightened me to see him begging to be left alone. One day Dr. Hill said: "We must get Hentz out of that room. I will see to it that he is put in a chair and rolled about the hospital. He has looked at those four walls long enough."

All of us were afraid to lift Hentz. It took the nurse, Margery, me, and two orderlies to get him into the chair. The first time he tried to sit up, he blacked out; but after ammonia and a temporary tilt backward he was all right. He couldn't hold his head up; and I wondered if he would ever be able to. We had to lean his head against the back of the chair and stuff pillows around it for support.

Every afternoon we would get him up for a tour of the

hospital. At first he wanted to visit the emptier parts of the building, but I was pleased when I noticed that each day he ventured farther. Before long the nurse was taking him to the hospital snack bar, and he would stop to talk to the switchboard operators, the janitors, the maids, the orderlies, and X-ray technicians.

He heard about a boy who had been seriously hurt in an accident. Someone told him of the boy's discouragement and defeatism. My heart swelled with pride when I heard him tell his nurse that he wanted to visit the boy during their afternoon stroll. He came back with a different look on his face, and I could see that he was losing some of his terrible self-consciousness.

We kept his forehead bandaged because it was an ugly sight. We never let Hentz see it. One day he asked to see it, and I told him that he'd better wait until we had had plastic surgery done on it. I told him frankly that he wouldn't like what he saw. People would stop and ask him what kind of accident he'd had because of the bandaged head. Giving any kind of answer was involved, but I think Hentz's nurse put off the curious ones by a firm and noncommittal manner.

Before long Hentz was visiting nearly all the patients in the hospital during the time he was in the chair. When the patients could walk they would repay his visits. They always told Charles Bledsoe and me how much it meant to them to have Hentz visit them; invariably they insisted that his visit had speeded their recoveries.

When the young people in Perry knew that Hentz was allowed to sit in a chair, they asked us if they could hold one of their Youth Fellowship meetings at the hospital. He was the president, and they thought it fitting and proper

that he be with them again. The superintendent of the hospital graciously offered the staff room for the meeting.

The twenty-five young people were hushed and quiet as
the nurse rolled Hentz into the room. Though they had seen
him in bed, this was the first time many of them had seen
him sitting up, and he looked thin and very frail. On every
face I saw wonder and admiration, and I prayed a quick
prayer that I wouldn't embarrass Hentz by crying. Seeing
him surrounded by young people who were so vigorous
and well, I wondered what was going on in his mind. Did
his smile hide bitterness? Did he watch the easy movements of
his active friends and grieve that his own body no longer
responded to his impulses? What, oh, what, did he hide behind that brave smile? Please, God, I prayed, don't let him
mind too much.

Everything went along smoothly. Fortunately, someone had
had the wisdom to plan the program with a light touch. After
a while they suggested singing the favorite songs of some of
those present. They turned to Hentz and told him to name
one he liked. His choice was a rather rousing, boisterous
Sunday-school song that he had always loved. There was
nothing especially inspiring about "Beulah Land," but it had
a catchy tune. When the music started I watched for his
reaction. He was singing! He had so little breath that it was
difficult for him to talk, but he was using his precious strength
to sing a song he loved. His eyes were moist, but he didn't
stop. I knew he must be remembering those other meetings
with these young friends when he was strong, and eager for
the services to end so that he could go somewhere with the
boys and girls. My pride in him knew no bounds, and I
thought of Tennyson's words, "Though much is taken much
abides."

After this meeting other groups came from Macon and other towns. Hentz always made his entrance serenely; and, thank goodness, none of the young people knew of the frantic scramble that was required to get him ready. There was always the fear that the orderlies would not be found when we needed them, and there was still the likelihood that Hentz would black out. Doing anything out of the ordinary created a great commotion in Room 231.

It was October, and Hentz was not really much improved. Though the doctors knew how the relentless waiting was eating away our hopes, and though they knew the terrible expense of the hospital and nurses, they were noncommittal still.

One night I went to the chart desk at the corner of the hall and stood talking to one of the nurses as she wrote in the ledger where the patients' names are listed. There were many names on the two pages of the opened book, but one stood out from the others.

I asked, "Why are all the other names written in black ink and Hentz's name in red?"

With no thought that it would frighten me, she gave me the information I sought. "Because his condition is still listed as critical."

After that I was afraid of the book. If I had to go to the desk about anything, and the nurse was writing, I would keep my head turned for fear I'd see my son's name written in red ink. My confidence that the doctors felt hope about Hentz was destroyed by a line in a thumb-worn ledger.

Dr. Hill and Dr. Taft called in a surgeon, Dr. Stevenson, to see the pressure sore. He had studied in New York and had done brilliant work since practicing in Macon. He said he had a procedure in mind if we could build Hentz up. If

successful it would close the ulcer immediately. I was afraid
he meant plastic surgery. I didn't want that because Mrs.
Van Diviere had told us how long it takes to heal. The
patient can't lie on his back, or sit for months. The doctors
advised us to bring Hentz home to see if a change of atmosphere and cooking would make him eat better.

Before he was hurt, Hentz's room was upstairs. Because
it was now out of the question to have him upstairs, I took
the dining-room furniture out and converted that room into
makeshift hospital quarters. The nurse would sleep in a
smaller bedroom downstairs.

Great was the confusion at the House of Houser for the
first time since May—it was now the latter part of October.
For the first time, since that May day, I stayed home from the
hospital to see that everything was in order. My next-door
neighbor and I painted the shutters on the house, for I didn't
want Hentz to see them faded. The best painter in town
painted Hentz's new room. When we asked how much we
owed him, he said: "Not one penny. I want to do that for
Hentz."

The house looked eager and alive after the dreadfully quiet
months. There were new chintz draperies in the nurse's room
that my neighbors made. There were flowers in every con-
ceivable spot. And the food! There were not enough places to
store the wonderful things our friends brought—and I knew
that if we ate all of it there wouldn't be room for us! Fred was
already getting rotund from the midnight snacks he, Hentz,
and the nurses had had at the hospital.

The great day came! I left Perry early to help Margery
and the nurse pack the huge accumulation of paraphernalia.

I left the hospital alone, before the others, to see about
some last-minute arrangements at home. When I neared our

house, I saw people everywhere! Every inch of the lawn was occupied by young people sitting on the grass, waiting patiently. As I pulled into our driveway they leaped to their feet. Some made a dash for the front steps. As I got closer, I saw music stands in position with open sheets of music. My throat constricted when I knew the band was there.

I went on into the house and peeped out every now and then at the scene in front. Older people were gathering in the street. The superintendent had let the entire high school out for this event, and people who had long been out of school also lingered to watch. I stayed inside because there were women coming and going all the time, still bringing beautifully arranged trays of food.

Suddenly I heard the music! I dashed to the nearest window. Fred, Margery, and Hentz had stopped in the driveway. Hentz was propped up among pillows on the front seat.

My boy had come home! I couldn't crowd out of my mind the picture I had originally had of his homecoming: Hentz walking up the front steps, confident and erect! I had thought that by this time he would be well. I had never imagined that he'd be the thin, pale boy that I could see between the slats of the blinds. In one way this day seemed to be a contradiction of our faith and hope. I turned from the window when I could bear to look no longer, and into the understanding arms of my husband's mother.

After a moment I steeled myself to go back to the window. I would fight my weakness, and the luxury of weeping. Now I could say, "Welcome home, son!" I looked at the members of the band, puffing and blowing, putting their hearts into this great salute. They rolled their eyes to the sides of their heads trying to see Hentz, and only occasionally rolled them back again to the music on the stands. Who cared if they

made a mistake? I didn't. All that mattered then was that
they were playing "Hail to the Chief" with all their hearts!
Hail to the chief! How wonderful! An inaugural parade
couldn't have inspired them more than the boy in the car
who refused to die—not once, but time and time again!

When I looked around at the women in the room, there
were no dry eyes.

Fred drove the car to the back yard. Hentz would have to
be transferred to his wheel chair, and he would not want
people to watch him while this was being done. Several men
helped Fred to make the change. I watched while Margery
put the final pats on his pillows and smoothed his hair. I was
composed, now, and I went outside to be with them. Margery
rolled the chair along, and Fred followed. The band was
playing "Dixie" now.

We rounded the corner of the house, and then the crowd
saw Hentz! Suddenly there was bedlam—the bedlam that only
youth knows how to create. Amid the shouting and cheering
and cries of "Welcome home!" and "Bravo!" Margery pushed
the chair over the rough flagstone walk toward the front
of the house. As I watched Hentz's tense face and dimmed
eyes, I had a terrible feeling of apprehension. I feared that
the welcome would prove too much of an emotional strain
for him, and that he would break down before this crowd
of people. How he would hate himself! I remember breathing
a quick prayer for him to keep his composure. My own
emotions made me afraid for him, but I should have known
that he would have control of himself in any situation.

As I anxiously watched him, I saw the old twinkle come
back to his eyes. A sudden hush came over the crowd as he
made a great effort to straighten his body. It was futile; but
he *could* raise his chin! Those nearest him heard him chuckle,

and say in a firm voice: "Maybe I won't ever be President, but let me tell you this: if my kidneys hold out, some day I'll be Governor of Georgia!

Being home was a mixed blessing. Fred could sleep in a bed again, and I could stay home from the hospital. But it was difficult for me to manage a house again—especially a house that had been so disorganized. A colored woman who had worked for us when Hentz was a little boy offered to help us out, and it was good to have someone to attend to the household matters.

The women of the different churches took turns giving showers for us. Hentz couldn't understand it. Though he had been sick so long, the attention never ceased. Many times he asked, "Why are they so good to me?"

Margery came to our house every morning to massage and exercise Hentz. She stayed until after lunch. Whenever we asked when she was going to return to Africa, she'd answer: "When Hentz goes to New York. I'll wait." Oh, it was good to have her! And, in spite of my conscience, I was glad she was adamant about staying.

I don't know what we thought would take place in New York; but everything we did was with the idea of hastening the day when Hentz could go to the Institute of Physical Medicine and Rehabilitation. Mrs. Van Diviere told us of men being made to walk who had been bed invalids for years. I believe now that she meant that they walked with braces and canes; but she said they walked, and we wanted to believe it.

Hentz had so much company that the nurse put a sign on the front door announcing visiting hours. We didn't like it, but I suppose it was necessary. We always feared we might miss someone especially interesting and entertaining. One day, during visiting hours, I answered a knock on the door. A bright-faced man of about forty-one asked if he could see Hentz. He introduced himself and said he'd had the same injury that Hentz had. I could hardly believe him because he looked so strong and erect.

I liked him at once and invited him into Hentz's room. He told us about his accident. He had fallen from a five-story building and had not only broken his neck, but his back also—and suffered concussions as well. He said that he had been paralyzed completely for over two years, and that he had not even been able to move his arms.

He told us of his many trials; of the visits from one doctor to another; of the pessimism of everyone—except his mother. He spoke of the love and attention of his family, and of his mother's unceasing prayers. He said she prayed to live to see him walk again. And she did. He certainly must have been telling the truth, because he was familiar with every phase of the hospitalization and treatment.

He turned to me and said, "Ma'am, if I live to be a hundred I'll never forget the first time I passed my water." That jarred me a little then, but a year later I could have discussed the matter with him with greater understanding.

Our visitor then rose from his chair and dramatically kicked one leg high over his head. "See? Nothing wrong with me now! I'm not stiff in any joint." When I asked him if there had been any deformities, he looked at me as if I were crazy, and said: "Lady, I was a mess! When I first started getting the feeling back and began to move a little, I was bent in the shape of an 'S.' I had to walk on my tiptoes because my feet had drawn back. My mother got me straight and limber again."

I wondered what magic his mother had used, and of course he was eager to tell me. "You know what red wigglers are? Fishing worms?" he inquired.

Though I knew what they were, I knew little else about them, because to me a worm is the most loathsome of all things created. I wondered if his mother had used them as doctors of another day used leeches.

"Well," he continued, "Mamma had somebody bring her a quart of red wigglers. She put them in a quart fruit jar and closed the lid tight. Then she put the jar of worms in a pot of boiling water and boiled them for several hours—the way you do beefsteak for sick folks. The worms made a salve when they was cooked a long time, and she used the salve to rub my stiff joints with. You sure ought to get some for your boy. Keep him from getting stiff."

I don't suppose he noticed how pale I turned. My stomach did a flip, and Hentz looked at me and laughed. I told Hentz later that if I *knew* for a positive fact that such treatment would make him walk, then I would do it for him—but that every element of doubt would have to be removed before I could put my hands to any such wonder-working emollient!

When I told several doctors about our visitor later, they were skeptical, and thought he was lying. I don't think so. He would have had to experience the things he talked about. Lying or not, he did us a lot of good.

After two weeks at home, where we were surrounded by friends and food, we went back to the hospital. Hentz was obviously improved, and had gained weight. We didn't mind going back, because to return meant progress.

CHAPTER EIGHT

The doctors, pleased with Hentz's improvement, went ahead with their plans for surgery. The surgeon made drawings for days of the ulcer on Hentz's back. He studied every possible phase of the proposed procedure.

The day of the operation—or, rather, operations—came. The urologist planned to put a tube into Hentz's bladder through the abdominal wall at the same time that the back operation was performed. The doctors asked Margery to go to the operating room with Hentz. They planned to use a very light anesthetic, and I knew she could help make him comfortable in body and mind. I wish she could always go with me through any dark places that might be waiting ahead.

The surgeon closed the ulcer by making it into a huge letter S lying in a horizontal position. Hentz had lost so much weight that the doctor was able to pull the flesh down on one side to cover the big wound and up on the other side. The scar must be eighteen or twenty inches long. There was much interest among the doctors about the operation, and many of them came to Hentz's room to see the closed wound. I didn't fully appreciate its importance until later. When we were finally in New York, I knew what the surgeon's skill had spared my son. I saw men who had been lying on their stomachs for months, some for over a year, while plastic surgery was being done on similar ulcers. If the wound had not been closed, Hentz could not have lived. The doctors said nobody could eat enough to replenish what was lost from the body through such pressure sores.

Margery told me some of the things the surgeon said in the operating room, and she came out feeling grateful for the skill and dedication of men like him. She said that somebody had begun discussing the staggering expense Fred had, and that the surgeon had said: "I'll never send a bill, or accept payment for anything I've done. Neither will Dr. Hill nor Dr. Taft nor Dr. Blanton. [Dr. Blanton was the anesthesiologist who had been with Hentz during all of his surgery. He had to lie on the floor for hours under the Foster bed.] The four of us feel that this is more than one man should be called on to bear—financially and in every other way. We believe that everybody is in something like this together. This is the least we can do." How like Margery he must have sounded!

There was never a time when we needed any of the doctors that they did not come willingly—regardless of the hour. They never seemed out of patience with any of us. Dr. Hill was with Hentz about an hour every night supervising the turning on the Foster bed, and trying to make Hentz comfortable. He would try anything Hentz suggested in an effort to make things easier. He designed swings and pulleys, casts and gadgets of every description. If they failed to work, he discarded them and patiently set to work on something different. His warmth and utterly delightful wit and sense of humor made his visits the highlight of the day.

Dr. Hill knew how much we wanted to believe that Hentz

would recover. He uttered no word, after that first night, that would discourage us. He would not tell us encouraging things to make us feel a false hope, and remained silent during the very critical periods. I remember something he said one night that lightened our burden. Margery had been exercising Hentz's legs, and she told Hentz to concentrate on moving a certain muscle. Several times she felt it move when she requested the effort. She didn't want to tell me because she knew I would begin to hope too much. When Dr. Hill came, she took him into the hall and told him. He had confidence in Margery, and knew she wouldn't imagine such an occurrence. I heard him say to her, "Anybody who says that Hentz can't recover is either a fool or a charlatan." Then he told us how doctors arrive at their conclusions— by statistics based on previously injured patients. I knew that Dr. Hill couldn't make such a statement if he knew that Hentz's spinal cord was severed. He looked at me and said: "Doctors look at cold figures, but there are times when what has happened before has no meaning. The events since Hentz's accident seem to fall into some kind of plan, and it is difficult to believe it is by chance or happen-so. At first nobody could have made me believe he would live. Now I can believe anything."

On the way home that night Margery and I went over every word he had said. We knew we were very fortunate to have such a man with Hentz. When I reached the house I could hardly wait to get to my room to pour out my gratitude to God. Dr. Hill hadn't really committed himself as to his prognosis, but what he said had overtones of hope. It was good to say "Thank you" to God because of something that made the future look brighter, and not just because God had let us get through another day. I never forget to express my gratitude, even when the day has been burdensome. I was thankful for each day that Hentz lived. Even on the most terrible days there would be something which I could cherish. That day I could believe that Dr. Hill felt hope.

Just before we took Hentz to New York we had the three Macon doctors and their wives to dinner in Perry. I was told later of a conversation that took place during their ride back to Macon. They were discussing Hentz, and one of the doctors said: "I had gotten pretty far away from God, and religion played a small part in my thinking. Knowing Hentz, and seeing at close range his faith and courage, and the faith of all concerned, has brought me closer to God than I've been in years." The others admitted that the experience had done the same for them.

When Hentz had recovered sufficiently from the back and bladder operations, the surgeon said he wanted to do some plastic surgery on his forehead. It still had not healed, and the doctor felt that for medical reasons the wound should be closed. He said that a place no larger than the one on Hentz's forehead could drain away the body's protein. So we sent him to the operating room again. This time we were glad to see him go, because he was making definite progress. With the big ulcer closed and the place on the forehead patched up, we might be getting closer to the yearned-for trip to New York.

One morning, many days after the operations, the surgeon was in Hentz's room changing the dressing. Before I realized what was happening, he had asked the nurse to hand him a mirror. I wanted to cry out to the doctor not to show it to Hentz, to wait until time had improved it! But I couldn't utter a word. He would think I was a silly woman trying to baby someone who'd proved that he was a man. I cringed as I saw the look in my son's eyes when he viewed his head for the first time since the injury had occurred. Horror, disgust, and revulsion were written on his face at what he saw in the mirror that was proudly held by the doctor. Hentz had never known how large this wound was, nor how, before the plastic surgery, it had eaten into his head until his skull was exposed.

I said, "Dr. Stevenson, tell him that time will improve the appearance of it." I tried to keep the urgency out of my voice.

"Oh, yes. Later on that patch in the middle will get blood vessels in it and look like the skin around it." Hentz remained silent.

The nurse followed the doctor out of the room. After they had left, Hentz turned to me and said: "As long as I live I don't want to talk about my head. I don't mind discussing any other phase of my illness, but I don't want anybody ever to mention my head to me. Please remember that. I don't want it mentioned in my presence, ever."

I hoped I would be given the wisdom to cope with his bitterness. I knew it would be impossible to prevent people from mentioning his forehead. I also knew that Hentz mustn't create a situation that would only mean additional hurt to him. I was hurt, too, by the change in his fine facial features. I suppose I admired his features more than he did. I said to him: "Son, anything that you try to shut up inside you gets worse and worse. Please don't build a wall of silence about your forehead. Talk about it, and you will find that it is easier to bear."

Later on, when the student nurses dropped by for a little visit, they remarked about the missing bandage. I was glad that the first ones to see his forehead were people who felt a professional interest and not an emotional one. They told him they thought it looked fine—or would before long.

As the surgeon promised, time has made the wound less noticeable. Hentz is still self-conscious about it, but he can speak of it, and that is fortunate, because many people comment on it. Later, we hope to have more plastic surgery done.

It seems that it took a long time for me to accept, without emotion, all the changes in our way of life, and in the way of life for Hentz. Each small change represents a great wrench at my heartstrings. Repetition has a way of making the ugliness of words and situations bearable, but it isn't an easy process.

One December day, not long before Christmas, I rolled Hentz to the front part of the hospital, while the nurse gathered up some clean linen and attended to other matters. I loved to go with him, but I knew he preferred the nurse. He didn't want people to think that Mother had to tag along, but I was happy when I was elected to roll the chair. Hentz was sitting in the wheel chair near the entrance watching the people and the cars go by. The wheel chair was old and clumsy and uncomfortable—one the hospital had had for a long time. The seat was polished wood, and the pillows had a maddening way of sliding on the smooth surface and causing Hentz to get in the wrong position. He was quiet, and I decided I wouldn't try to talk to him.

In a little while he rolled his head on his pillow so that he was facing me. In a strained voice he said, "Mother, do you know what I want for a Christmas present?"

I wondered what it could be that made him speak so strangely. I felt a sudden lift of spirit to know there was something he could think of that friends hadn't already provided. There was so little he could use.

With a great effort to sound casual, he continued, "If they aren't too expensive, I'd like a nice wheel chair." His voice shook a little. It was the first time he had hinted that he thought his condition would not soon be changed.

For a moment I couldn't answer. I knew his heart was crying out for me to tell him that the doctors didn't think one would be necessary. My heart didn't want to believe that one was necessary. Surely our prayers would be answered before long! At last I said: "The very idea! You won't need a wheel chair long—but if you want one you shall certainly have it."

The Van Divieres heard that Hentz was sitting up, and a few days later they came to the hospital with the fine custom-made chair their son had used. I felt very strange as I heard Hentz exclaim with joy at the chair's beauty. How could my boy, who a few months ago had been so vigorous, now find beauty in a wheel chair?

As the anxious days grew into weeks and months, we all learned to be natural about wheel chairs and about a great number of objects that had never had a place in our existence before. On the occasion when Hentz came home from the hospital for the first time, the wheel chair remained in the living room when it was not in use. Every time I entered the room it was all I could see. No matter how hard I tried not to look at it, I saw it. Though I never walked close to it, I couldn't get away from it. It was the inanimate symbol of all the suffering and hopes and prayers of the months past— the prayers answered and the ones yet to be answered. Now, when I go into the room where the chair is, it is no more offensive than any other article of furniture.

Hentz's birthday is December 12th, and it was apparent that he would still be in the hospital. A few days before the date some girls from Perry asked me if he would be able to attend a surprise party if the hospital would let them have one. Bless the dear old Macon Hospital! They said the young people could have the nurses' and doctors' dining room immediately following the lunch hour. They could do their decorating between lunch and dinner and have the party after the dinner was finished.

On the afternoon of the twelfth droves of young people came. They were laden with crepe paper, horns, balloons, and other material. They wouldn't go into Hentz's room in large groups, but all afternoon there was a constant stream of smaller groups visiting him. We had warned every soul in the hospital, from the janitor in the basement to the superintendent, not to breathe a word to Hentz about the great plans. I had decided to be very extravagant and get a real artist to make Hentz's cake. I told the young people that I wanted to provide the cake. There is a woman in Perry who does the prettiest confectionery work I've ever seen, and I requested that she make this one the finest cake ever.

On the morning of the twelfth Margery and I went by to get the cake to take to the hospital. When we looked upon her creation, we could hardly believe it was real. Over the immense white three-tiered cake she had spread bright, festive poinsettias. How glad I was that she had the good sense to know that they would be more appropriate than sweetheart roses twined around "Happy Birthday"! The cake was a sensation, and everyone had to touch it before he could believe that the poinsettias were not real. I was humbled when she wouldn't let me pay her for it. She said it gave her pleasure.

The young people had fun stringing up the "Happy Birthday, Hentz," the letters having been cut out of foil. Hundreds of birthday cards were put on strings to make swags, and banked on shelves.

Hentz knew something unusual was taking place: we couldn't fool old fox! He knew that that many of his friends wouldn't decide to go shopping in Macon on the same day.

The entire hospital knew about the party, even the patients. Everyone who was able walked to the dining room to see the frantic preparations.

Hentz didn't feel well; he had had a chill before the party, and his fever was higher than usual. He was never free of fever; but at times, when his bladder was giving trouble, his fever went very high. The urologist had chosen that day to change the tube in the bladder, and there was always a reaction from that. But we crossed our fingers and hoped for the best.

The time came for him to make his appearance. I've forgotten what ruse we used to get him into the chair at such an unusual hour. Fred and I, his mother and my mother, relatives and friends had preceded Hentz and the nurse to the dining room. We hid in the rear of the big room so that we could observe Hentz's face when he saw the sight. Such occasions were a mixture of distress and joy to me. The joy came from people's great desire to bring happiness to my son; the distress stemmed from my knowledge that such times must make him more conscious of his changed way of life. Over a hundred young people from Macon and Perry were there, excited and eager.

Everyone felt repaid. In Hentz's feverish eyes they saw gratitude. He tried desperately to show the enthusiasm he felt; but a few minutes after he entered the room he whispered something to his nurse, and she quickly rolled him out of the room. Though he was taken to a room where there were several windows, in spite of the fresh air and a whiff of ammonia he blacked out. The urinary infection, with the accompanying fever, as well as the excitement and heat in the dining room, were too much. He sent word to the young people to go on with the fun and forget about him. But before long I saw the nurse bringing him back to the party. My admiration and respect for him were never greater. I knew the effort he was making to stay up, and I knew that he should be back in bed. But I also knew that there was no need to tell him to leave.

That is how Hentz spent his eighteenth birthday.

With a sameness that should have been monotonous, but wasn't, the days came and went until the Christmas season arrived. Each day was one more with no sign that the paralysis that stilled my son was lessening. We had an antenna put on the hospital so that he could have a television set in his room. Since that day I have wished that every sick person in the world could have one! What a delightful way to bring new faces into the sick room! No matter how kind and loving the old faces are, they can become monotonous. With a TV the patient can see pretty faces, clever faces, sincere ones and funny ones. Nothing we've ever bought for him means what the TV means. I think we could do without the stove, refrigerator, sink, and bathtub easier than we could do without the TV.

Hentz was still getting the Pyromen, on which we had pinned so much hope. It had to be administered intravenously, and the interns had increasing difficulty finding the veins. The drug added a degree or two of fever to the fever he ordinarily had, and it caused him to feel very warm. In his corner room were two immense windows, and he insisted that they be raised as high as they would go, in addition to having an electric fan going full blast. Now, I love cold weather, but sitting all day in that room in December was a real test for my maternal devotion. The nurse provided me with the strange cotton leggings they put on patients before they go to the operating room. I wore a coat all day, tied a scarf round my head, and kept on gloves, which were troublesome when I was turning pages of a book. Hentz thought I was being ridiculous, and he refused to believe that the weather was cold. None of his visitors could withstand the rigors of Room 231 except for a few brief moments; then I would take them to the cot in the hall to thaw them out.

All hope was gone that we could spend Christmas at home. The doctors still shook their heads when we asked. Hentz was better now: of that we were certain. He was stronger, and could hold up his head in the chair. He gained weight and strength rapidly when the ulcers were closed. The doctors said New York might be a reality before long. "Be patient. Be patient," I tried to tell my heart.

Fred said I had made Hentz's room too gaudy, but I insist that you can't be too gaudy at Christmas. I put everything that friends sent to the hospital in the way of Christmas decorations in the room. It really was a mess, and the nurse couldn't find anything she needed; but I was determined that this was to be the most decorated Christmas anybody in a hospital ever had! As long as the decorations came, I found a place to display them. We put up tables in the hall for Hentz's presents, and I began to suspect that our wonderful friends had the same idea in mind that I did.

A few days before Christmas, Warren and Mattilu Hodge came by the hospital to visit Hentz. Warren told Hentz that he had a wonderful Christmas present for him—something no patient had ever received in a hospital. I was a little apprehensive, knowing Warren as I did. By this time he was at his home, able to eat, talk, see, laugh—everything but walk.

Things were pretty quiet at the hospital that Christmas Eve. I suppose everyone was home decorating and cooking and running to stores for last-minute items. I tried to crowd out of my memory the other Christmases. Don't look back, I said to myself. Live this minute, and live it well. Margery was working with Hentz, and I was reading, when someone knocked on the door. When I opened it I saw a man who was not dressed in city clothes, and quite obviously nervous. He asked, "Is this Hentz Houser's room?" and I said it was. "I have a present for him, something Mr. Hodge had me bring." With that he dashed furtively down the hall. I thought his behavior was a little peculiar, but attributed it to the fact that he might not be familiar with hospitals.

In a little while he knocked again, and I opened the door. He and a frightened-looking colored man were holding an orange crate in their arms. There was a paper lining inside the crate, and we couldn't see the contents. The two men put the orange crate on the floor of Hentz's room and hurriedly made their exit.

Hentz and Margery asked me to remove the paper so that they could see what was in the box. I started tearing at the paper through the wooden slats. With the first tearing, rattling sound a noise came from the box that sent me, startled, across the room.

"Ba-a-a-h! Ba-a-a-h!" Never has there been a noise so penetrating and so plaintive as that which came from that frightened but beautiful baby billy goat!

After the first delighted shock of seeing the little fellow, we realized we had a problem on our hands. The hospital had been wonderful to us through many peculiar things we had done, but we had the notion that a goat would tax their leniency too far. The poor little animal jumped from chair to chair, and from corner to corner. I knew he was scared, so I patted him and talked baby talk to him, and he formed a great affection for me. I had to continue patting him to keep him from making any more of those awful noises! I tried to feed him, but he didn't like the fare and seemed to prefer to munch on the plastic leather covering on the big chair.

In the afternoon, when it was time for the nurse to take Hentz in his chair for his tour of the hospital, I decided to go too. I got partway down the hall when I heard the goat! How could such a little thing make so much noise? I dashed back to the room and promised him I wouldn't leave him again. And I didn't. I didn't dare. The superintendent came by to inquire how things were with us, and I was terrified for fear the goat would make a noise or move out from under the bed.

Somehow the news slipped out that Hentz had a goat in his room, and the nurses and interns came to see for themselves. I didn't know what to do with the little fellow: I didn't have a car in Macon because Fred had gone back to Perry in it. There was nothing to do but wait until eight o'clock, when Fred got there, and decide on some course of action.

He and Leonora and Louise came into the room with their usual glad and rather noisy hello, and this set the little goat off again. Fred delivered quite a tirade. What would we do with it? We would be thrown out of the hospital! But I knew he thought it was cute. After I quieted the little thing again, I told Fred about the strange attachment the goat had for me.

Fred said: "There's nothing strange about it at all. He loves the familiar smell."

"But, Fred, we can't make him eat anything! I'm so worried because he hasn't had a thing all day."

Fred looked at the little goat scampering over the chairs and stools, and said: "It isn't his intake that *I'm* worried about. It's his output."

Shortly afterward Dr. Taft came for his evening visit with Hentz. With a beseeching look we asked him if he didn't want the goat for his four adorable little boys. He took to the idea immediately. Next we called Warren to ask him if we could give the goat to Dr. Taft. Warren thought it was an excellent idea, but made one stipulation. We had to name the goat Henry, for Dr. Taft. Warren had been one of his patients, and their admiration was mutual.

Dr. Taft and Fred gently put Henry in the crate after fixing the paper lining back in place. The little fellow didn't make a sound. Fred and the doctor were pleased because they felt sure they could get to the car without being discovered. They picked him up and started down the hall with him, still quiet. A student nurse in the chart room at the corner knew about the goat, and when they passed her she thrust her hand through the slats, and said, "Goodbye, little goat." With that he gave a tremendous farewell "Ba-a-a-h!" That was enough to bring heads out of doors down the length of the hall, and on other floors too.

If the superintendent and the others in authority knew about Henry, they never said anything. They were kind people, and very understanding.

On Christmas morning I left Perry very early, laden with more presents for all of us. I wanted to get to the hospital

as soon as Hentz waked up. He mustn't have too much time
to think. He mustn't remember the other Christmases when
he and I ran to the living room before daylight to see what
Santa Claus had brought us, yelling all the while for Fred to
wake up and look in his stocking. Sleep was more precious to
Fred than anything Santa could put in his stocking, but it
always vexed us that he felt so. When I reached the hospital
Hentz hadn't been awake very long, and he showed interest
in the gifts I had brought. Fred and I were humbled—a daily
occurrence—by the goodness of people. Throughout the
unwrapping of packages, I silently said, "Thank you, God,
for letting Hentz live to see Christmas."

Dr. Taft came to report on Henry's reception. He said: "It
seems that Henry was a wise choice. I could have saved
all the money I spent on the other presents for the boys. They
didn't see a thing but that goat! When they went into the
living room to see what Santa had brought them, the goat
was in my wife's best chair!"

When all the packages had been opened there was nothing
to do but wait for the Christmas dinner. The dietitian had
said she wanted us to be the guests of the hospital, and have
Christmas dinner in the room with Hentz. There is so little
to do at a hospital on holidays! Hentz was very quiet, and
all my efforts to make him talk failed. Fred told some of his
long-winded jokes, which usually brought remonstrances
and entreaties for mercy; but this time Hentz didn't try to
stop him. Fred told his long jokes to the end—a rare
happening—and I tried to laugh when he finished one.

Someone called Fred out of the room, and I looked at
Hentz. His head was turned away from me on his pillow.

Though I walked around the bed and stood close to him, I didn't speak. I saw tears on his cheeks.

I didn't ask him what was wrong. Perhaps he had set Christmas as the deadline when he would be well. Without wanting to, I remembered Philip in Maugham's *Of Human Bondage*. Why did I have to think of him on Christmas? There were too many hurtful things in the present to think of, without remembering the ones that were old. When I read the book, so may years ago, I suffered with young Philip when he prayed so terribly hard for God to make his clubfoot whole; and I shared his shattering grief when he knew that the miracle had not taken place. I understood his growing bitterness because he had believed that with sufficient faith he could remove mountains. He felt cheated and tricked.

The prayer I prayed as I looked at Hentz was: "Please, God, don't let Hentz know the kind of disappointment that Philip felt. Don't let Hentz become bitter, as Philip did."

Hentz was ashamed because I had seen his tears, and he turned his head away from me again. He had needed to cry for a long time—my boy who was a man.

"Cry. Cry if you want to. We'll lick it! Some day things will be different!"

But he wouldn't cry—not even on Christmas. With his jaw firmly set, he looked at me and said: "Who wants to cry? There's nothing to cry about!"

Fred came back, and before long the dietitian brought Christmas dinner. Hentz didn't want anything then, and promised to eat a hamburger later on.

I think we must have looked strange sitting there amid all the wreaths, miniature trees, holly, Christmas ornaments, and Santa Clauses. My Christmas tray was on the table by

Hentz's bed, surrounded by medicines, and Fred was trying to balance his on his knees while sitting on a footstool.

I cut a piece of the turkey and had my fork in mid-air when Fred said, "Don't you think we had better say a blessing?"

I put the fork down and bowed my head. Part of the gesture was because of the shame I felt.

I had forgotten.

CHAPTER NINE

One especially beautiful bright day between Christmas and January 1, 1952, Hentz came home from the Macon Hospital. We were waiting now for word from the University Hospital in New York that there was a bed available. The doctors in Macon said we could wait as well in Perry, and we knew Hentz would be happier and eat better.

Now that we were so close to the dream, waiting was burdensome. Hentz was impatient. We still had not learned how much time slips away from people with spinal cord injuries.

Hentz was able to go out in the car now, but we knew so little about handling him. We didn't have a nurse this time. We had an untrained colored boy to help with the lifting. When we took Hentz for rides in the car Fred would have to come home from the office, and call two or three of the strong neighbors—it took five of us to get him in the car. I don't think the rides gave Hentz very much pleasure because of the difficulty we had moving him.

All the details of the stay in New York were settled, and every few days Mr. Sanders, the counseler from the Georgia Vocational Rehabilitation Department, came to see us. The

State of Georgia was going to pay Hentz's expenses in the New York hospitals. Mr. Sanders had visited us so often that by now we considered him one of our good friends. His quiet assurance and belief that much could be done for Hentz helped our morale. I remembered the first time I had met him, and how distressed I had been at his talk about rehabilitation.

Mr. Sanders never discussed the cost of the rehabilitation in my presence. There were no embarrassing questions, or any suggestion that we had to be indigent to receive the help they offered. Fred told me that he had to make a financial statement; but I suppose that by the time Hentz finished his hospitalization in Macon, the statement was not impressive. Fred and I didn't discuss our financial situation: we had so little time together, and when we were at the hospital we were in Hentz's room trying to make him laugh, or at the little snack bar. I know we mortgaged the house because I had to sign some papers, but knew no other details. There were worries so much greater than money worries. I didn't want to ask Fred about such matters, and he didn't want to burden me with them. I always knew that somehow we would manage, and I don't remember ever having any concern about money. A hospitalization of eight months, with nurses, surgery, costly drugs and medications, and transfusions, is expensive. Mr. Sanders knew, as did all the others with the department, that the injury Hentz had suffered was very expensive to treat. He must have known, on the first day I met him, that by the time Hentz was physically able to go to New York we would hardly be financially able to send him. We had never had to accept anything from anybody in our lives, and I had always thought that to do so would deal a fatal blow to our pride and self-respect.

But every detail had been handled so carefully and so considerately that our pride did not suffer. We have never asked for anything—it has not been necessary: they have anticipated our needs.

While we waited in Perry, Margery lovingly and quietly worked with Hentz every day. I don't know what we would have done without her. We depended on her for so much else in addition to the treatment she gave Hentz. When we received the message from New York to be there on February 5th, she made her plans to go to New York in order to return by ship to her duties abroad. The idea of taking Hentz to New York was so wonderful that I could hardly believe it had actually been settled; but the thought of not having Margery saddened us even in the midst of our joy.

The day we left was one of glad turmoil! Many people came to see us off, and it was comforting to know that they cared enough to get up very early in the morning to wish us well. They stood around watching while Hentz was rolled into the ambulance for the ride to Atlanta to get the plane. Fred and I climbed in last, the door was closed, and we could no longer see the good faces and the waving hands of our friends.

The Housers were on their way to the Promised Land.

Some of the personnel from the Vocational Rehabilitation Department were at the airport when we arrived in Atlanta. They had arranged for our ambulance to be driven on the field near the plane. They asked that we sit in the little room behind the pilot's room that they called the Sky Room.

A photographer from the Vocational Rehabilitation Department snapped several pictures of Hentz on the rolling stretcher. I asked Fred in a whisper if he thought they'd publish the pictures. I knew that Hentz would not want such a picture in the paper. He looked so sick lying there, waiting to get on the plane. Fred said he didn't know. Then I thought: If we accept so much, we can't tell them what not to do. If there is a picture in the Atlanta papers of Hentz being flown to New York, I shall have to keep quiet. Little did I know then of the discerning judgment of the people who worked with the State of Georgia Rehabilitation Department.

The State had wired ahead for an ambulance to meet us at Newark. Before we reached Philadelphia, the weather grew very bad. When we arrived over Newark Airport the pilot came to our little room and told us that he could not make a landing because of bad weather, but that he would fly over the New York area hoping to find a hole in the fog. After we'd flown over New York for more than two and a half hours, the pilot came back to announce that he would have to return to Philadelphia. If I'd ever had any doubts about Hentz's desire to live, his reaction would have dissolved them. He looked relieved when he knew we would not try to land. He laughed, and said to the pilot: "I may look a mess, but I want to stick around a while. I'm not planning to stay this way forever." The pilot was greatly concerned because he knew of the ambulance that was waiting. Finally we asked the pilot to radio for an ambulance to meet us in Philadelphia in order to drive us to New York.

It was good to be on the ground again, and our enthusiasm was not dampened. However, the drive from Philadelphia to New York seemed very long and tedious. Hentz had been in a sitting position for several hours on the plane, and the surgeon in Macon had warned against too much pressure on the closed wound. Hentz enjoyed the ride because the driver was a great conversationalist, and gave us a vivid account of

Philadelphia politics, liberally sprinkled with "youse." Until then, Hentz hadn't believed people actually used the word.

With an intermingling of hope and uncertainty I got out of the ambulance and stood before the hospital. Twentieth Street looked deserted and remote in the drizzling rain. The street lights made long yellow streaks across the wet pavement. The University Hospital was crowded close to other buildings, and the air of spaciousness and airiness that I'd associated with the hospitals I'd known was missing. The night was raw, and penetrated the spring coat I was wearing.

As Fred and I followed the driver into the dingy basement entrance we encountered a kindly little old man. His neck and back were twisted from arthritis, and his hair was snowy white, but there was something about him—maybe patience, compassion, understanding or joy of overcoming—that I responded to. I felt less lonely and afraid. He showed the driver where to take Hentz; he seemed interested in us; and his gentleness made the next step seem less foreboding.

I hoped Hentz wouldn't have to stay here long. We had been informed that all patients who were to enter the Institute of Physical Medicine and Rehabilitation had to go through a routine examination. He would have to stay here for a few days only, and then he could go to the new building where they performed magical deeds for people like my son.

The Philadelphia ambulance driver rolled Hentz down the drab hall toward a chart room or office. A stern-faced nurse met us, looked at the boy on the stretcher, and then at Fred and me. "Your son? Is he a miner?"

"He's my son, and he is eighteen years old," I replied.

"I didn't mean that. Did he work in the mines?"

"He has never worked in a mine," I answered.

"Take him to the Miners' Ward," she said to the driver, "Fifth bed on the left." She gestured toward the ward, and waved her hands toward the stretcher as a farm woman does shooing chickens. I didn't argue about my son not being hurt in the mines, and thought if we were being sent to the wrong place it would soon be discovered.

Fred and I followed Hentz and the driver into the dreary ward. The other patients watched with feigned disinterest as Hentz was being put into bed. I could tell that some of them had seen many patients come and go, and we felt the vague discomfort of the uninitiated. As the ambulance driver started to go, I felt a twinge at the thought of losing somebody who seemed so close to us. The drive through the fog had made him familiar, and all else around us was so alien. I had a box of camellias I had brought from our yard, and I hurriedly opened it and gave the driver two of the lovely blooms. I said: "Thank you so much for everything. Please give these to your wife." His "Youse don't know how she'll love 'em" were the last words he said before waving a cheery goodbye.

A television set was at one end of the long room, and some of the patients were looking at it. Some were looking in the other direction with that "terrible patience" that my friend, Anne Griffin, dreaded to see Hentz develop.

An airy male nurse came to Hentz's bed and started talking. We had never seen a male nurse before. He said, "My name's Hennessy, and I'm on private duty with Sammy, the boy over there." He pointed to a young, dark-haired boy across the aisle who was lying on an orthopedic frame. "He broke his neck playing football six or eight months ago. He's in critical condition. I help all the boys in the ward, and if the kid needs anything"—he pointed to Hentz—"if he'll just yell I'll help him. I love all of 'em." He laughed, and he had no teeth. One of the patients yelled something to Hennessy about his teeth, and he said, "Aw, shaddup! I got teeth. I'll show ya!" He went to a window behind Sammy's bed and picked up a set of false teeth and held them high for everyone to see.

Hennessy came back across the room. I asked, "Is this called the Miners' Ward?"

"Yes—that's right." He answered cheerfully.

"Why? Are all the patients miners? My son wasn't."

"No?" He appeared interested. "Most of the patients in here worked in the mines, bless 'em."

If Fred and I could not stay with Hentz, I was glad he was in a ward. It was strange and dreary, and the people were not like any people we knew, but it was better than being alone in a private room in a strange hospital.

There were fourteen beds in the ward, and they were end to end with an aisle between them. I think all of the patients, with the exception of Sammy, Hennessy's patient, were on their stomachs, with their heads at the foot of the bed so that they could talk to the patient across the aisle, and see what was going on in their restricted little world. There were three stacks of pillows under each one of them. One stack was under the chest, another under the thighs, and the third one between the knee and ankle. They were in the process of having plastic surgery done on pressure sores on their backs. They ate, drank, read, and slept in that position. Some had been that way for months, and some for over a year. Sammy was the only other quadriplegic in the ward. The others were paraplegics—and it makes a great difference when the hands are not involved.

After we had given Hentz's history to a young Negro, and when all the other preliminaries were settled, I knew we would have to leave. I disliked the thought of leaving my son there, alone with strangers. It was the second night since his accident that one of us, or Charles, had not stayed with him. I knew he was courageous, but I also knew that the sudden removal of the great care and kindness to which he had become accustomed would be an emotional shock. I hoped his independence would not keep him from asking for the things he needed. He couldn't turn on the light above his bed to signal for help. He couldn't reach out for the water he needed. He couldn't fluff up a troublesome pillow, and he couldn't straighten the covers. Oh, my son, I hope all goes well with you, I thought as I looked at him. He might think himself a man, but at that moment he was my little boy who was hurt and far from home. I wanted desperately to kiss him and whisper that I loved him, but I was afraid. Before I got out of reach of the bed I patted his leg, hoping it would convey to him some of my love and concern, only to realize again, for the thousandth time, that he couldn't feel my touch. He was looking the other way.

Dr. Donald Covalt, who was then the Clinical Director, and who is now Associate Director, of the Institute of Physical Medicine and Rehabilitation, made an appointment with Fred and me to talk about Hentz. Ours was the first appointment of the day, and we were at the Institute on Thirty-fourth Street early. We sat in the lobby waiting for Dr. Covalt to arrive at his office. As we sat there the outpatients began to arrive for treatment. They came with attendants; they came rolling their own chairs, walking with Canadian canes, and swinging through on crutches. Regardless of the extent of their disability, they had one thing in common: their shining faces. I had never seen so many handicapped people at one time before. Suddenly I began to cry. If the patients had looked disgruntled and miserable, I would not have been as affected as I was by the joy on their faces. I wished I could look upon beauty without tears.

Dr. Covalt's secretary asked Fred and me to follow her. Dr. Covalt told us what they would try to do for Hentz. He gave us no false hope, nor was he discouraging. He said: "The muscular return limits what we can do. If Hentz gets more return, we can probably put him on crutches with long leg braces. If he does not get more return, we can teach him to do many things for himself. There is much in life for him if he wants to find it."

I said, "He'll find it!"

Dr. Covalt nodded. "In this work we find that determination is the most important factor. One of the most successful men I know is a man with only *one* muscle in his arm. With that one muscle he drives a specially designed automobile and runs one of the largest export-import businesses in the Southwest." Just as on the night that Dr. Hill told us that he'd known one person to live with an injury as serious as Hentz's, I knew that what any other man did Hentz could do.

Fred left New York after two days. The day after he left, the urologist examined Hentz, and found stones in his bladder which he removed. Then I was informed that he had six stones in his right kidney, and that they would have to be removed. They also planned to do a second operation on his bladder—it was called a transurethral resection. I dreaded to think of anything as major as kidney surgery in New York, away from all the people who had been so faithful. It was difficult, too, to have to make decisions alone. I had to sign for operations and do things that I had not done before. I had to try to replace the people who had been close to Hentz at home.

One day, when Hentz was in extreme pain, I whispered to him, "Whom the Lord loveth He chasteneth." Through the pain his sense of humor came through, but without disrespect: "Boy, how He must love me!" I never felt that God made Hentz suffer, although I believe that He could relieve him if I prayed and believed enough. Sometimes Hentz would say, "I wish I understood."

I wished I could help him understand, so I said: "Hentz, there are laws of God and laws of Nature, and when we violate them we pay the penalty. You knew the lake was too shallow—don't you remember hitting your head two or three days before you were injured? Remember that I warned you of the danger? You laughed, because you didn't think anything like that would happen to you. You defied the warning and broke one of Nature's laws."

Hentz said, "Several people have intimated that such things are punishment from God."

That reminded me of the man back home who said: "I think God is punishing your son for something, and that's why He let him break his neck. Don't you think so?" I was indignant, but I tried not to show it because the man was old.

I replied to the man: "I couldn't worship a God like that. I don't believe any such thing, and I don't understand how you can. Don't you think all of us would have broken necks if God meted out His punishment in such a manner? Hentz was not wicked, and God did not break his neck."

I kept one promise that Jesus made close to my heart. At first I did tell a few people about the comfort I derived from it, but without fail they began to rationalize and to attempt to explain that it didn't mean what it said. It is in Mark

11:24: *Therefore I say unto you, What things soever ye desire, when ye pray, believe that ye receive them, and ye shall have them.* There were no stipulations and no conditions to the promise. All we had to do was to believe. Nothing was said about our request being God's will: *"What things soever* ye desire."

Hentz was well into the routine of the hospital, and when he recovered sufficiently from the bladder operations they placed him on a board called a tilt board. He was bound to it by wide leather straps. Everyone was surprised when he didn't black out the first time they stood him in an upright position. He looked tall and very thin, and a little like an Egyptian mummy.

I was permitted to stay at the hospital so much that the patients became a part of my life. I worried when one of them was wheeled out of the ward to go to surgery, and when they came back I wanted to try to comfort and console them. They were so brave! There was no wife, mother, father, brother, or even a friend to wish them well when they left, and no one to stand by the bed and hold their hand and show their sympathy when they returned. One day Hentz received a letter from Dr. Stevenson in Macon, who said that Hentz had more "guts" than anybody he knew. Hentz said: "I don't know *any*thing about guts. Those other boys do. Going through big operations alone, as they do, takes guts."

At first the patients in the ward seemed suspicious of my attempts to be kind. I wanted to do little things for them, and never left the hospital without asking all of them if I could make some purchases before I returned. They didn't feel at ease with me until they were certain that my interest was sincere. When Hentz was first admitted, there was a precious old Russian, called Papa, across the aisle from him. He had worked in the mines, and the Miners' Association was taking care of his expenses. He looked like an extremely happy Popeye when he smiled. When he was in pain he cried like a child, but when the pain passed the smile returned. Though he wouldn't do the exercises the therapist ordered him to do, all of us protected Papa. No one could betray him when he smiled! Even the therapist was caught in the magic of it. One day they told Papa he was well enough to go to the Institute to begin to learn to walk with braces and canes. He didn't want to leave the hospital, and we heard later that he was very unhappy at the Institute without his old friends. One day Dr. Covalt asked me to go to see Papa if I had the time. I fixed him a box of candy, cigarettes, and cookies, and asked all the patients in the ward to write Papa a note.

Papa was very subdued when I walked into his room. I told him that I had come to bring him all the gossip from the hospital, and some little things to eat, but that, best of all, I had brought a message from everyone in the ward. Because he couldn't read English, he asked me to read the messages to him. Though some of them made me blush, I pretended not to notice, and read all of them. Papa's grin was ample reward.

After my visit to Papa the men in the ward began asking me to do little favors for them, such as buying razor blades, stamps, writing paper, and cigarettes. It made me happy to feel that I could help them a little—and happier that they felt free to ask me.

One day, as I was walking very fast down the hall, the woman doctor who was in charge of the ward stopped me.

I took a deep breath and braced myself for what she had to say.

She said: "I think you have about worked yourself into a job here. Are you at all interested in doing something? Dr. Covalt will be glad to pay well for it." I said that I didn't think I could consider a job because if Hentz needed me I wanted to be free. She went on to say that she wanted me to do something to keep the men in the ward occupied—not just making billfolds and things like that. She wanted their minds to be busy. She said she thought that Hentz and I might have some ideas. Rarely have I been more pleased; but such an assignment was out of the question. I wanted to help those men and boys more than anything in the world; but I knew that, as soon as I knew I was *supposed* to be entertaining, I would freeze up. I told her that I thought it would be better for everyone if I pleased them accidentally from time to time.

Friends in New York, and friends of friends, helped to make our stay there happier. I had a nephew, who lived in one of the New Jersey suburbs, whom I had not seen since he was a little boy. He visited the hospital every opportunity he had, and Hentz and I were devoted to him. Anne Griffin had friends who came to see us immediately after our arrival, and I knew they would keep coming. One of Anne's friends was Tracy Horton, of Atlanta, who was doing graduate work at Columbia. Anne had taught Tracy at Wesleyan College in Macon. Though much younger than I, I knew at once that Tracy would be a friend. The first time she visited Hentz and me at the hospital, she came with a young man named James Tanis, who was attending the Union Theological Seminary. James's father had been a Presbyterian minister, and James was planning his life so as to continue his father's work. James and Tracy usually visited us together, and they always brought some little something to brighten up the surroundings. They would buy daffodils, or a few roses, and arrange them in one of the old steins James collected.

A day or so after Tracy's first visit, another of Anne's friends called me to say that she wanted to come to my hotel. I had heard Anne talk about Lois Crews. She and her husband, Albert, were at Northwestern University when Anne was doing graduate work there. For the last few years they had been living in New York, where Albert worked as Director of the Television, Broadcasting and Film Commission, for the National Council of Churches of Christ in the U.S.A.

The moment I saw Lois get off the elevator, I knew I would like her. Because she had heard about us through Anne, she took my hands in both of hers and said, "Please, Harriet, tell me *everything*. I'm so anxious to hear." Before long I discovered that I *could* tell her everything. I felt none of the reserve and constraint that one usually feels with new acquaintances. While we were eating lunch in a cozy little tearoom that was decorated with antiques, I found that I could even tell her about the time Hentz's toes moved. She assured me that she understood, and believed. She had the kind of faith and trust that made me feel stronger; and it was good to be able to say some of the things I needed to say.

Having Lois and Albert and Tracy and James and my nephew, Bill Hentz, nearby made my stay in New York less lonely, and they tried very hard to replace our loved ones back home. They introduced me to their friends, and they and their friends visited Hentz. Before long New York was no longer a lonely place in which to live, but a town wherein I knew I had many good, sincere friends.

One morning during the latter part of February, I arrived at the hospital and found Hentz hemorrhaging from his bladder. Though the doctor worked with him all day, at midnight Hentz was still bleeding. The doctor, who was from Manila, had always seemed distant and inscrutable. He was the assistant to the urologist at the hospital, and everyone respected his knowledge and skill, but I had ceased to make any effort to be friendly to him. Whenever I spoke to him in the halls, I had the feeling that he'd rather not speak; after a while I would turn my head and pretend I didn't see him. But as he worked with Hentz, I was conscious only of his desire to stop the bleeding and to help my son. At midnight the doctor said: "You had better go to your hotel and try to get some rest. If things get worse I'll call you. I'm going to stay with Hentz all night." I wanted to stay; but I did as he suggested, knowing that Hentz was in good hands.

When I reached the hotel I called Fred. I was scared and tired, and not at all brave any more, and I needed to share some of my burdens with Fred. I begged him to come; but he said it was out of the question because it was near the end of the month and he had to be at his office. He told me that he would call his brother in Washington to go to New York to be with us.

Fred's brother, Parks, had been a prisoner of the Japanese for three and a half years. He was captured on Bataan, made the terrible Death March, and went hungry for years, yet managed to survive the torturous trip in a cattle boat from the Philippines to Korea, where he saw men die by the hundreds.

He watched while friends he'd had since the days at West Point went mad from the lack of water and air. He slept huddled on cold floors with his friends, and saw them die next to him during the night. But human life never became cheap to Parks. Actually, his experience made him more compassionate. I knew that if Fred could not come, his brother Parks would be the next best choice.

As I entered the ward next morning, I saw a tall figure in Army clothes. Parks was standing by Hentz's bedside. Opposite him was the Filipino doctor. I was so relieved to see that they were talking pleasantly: Hentz must be better.

Hentz was not better, however, and in a few hours he was taken to the operating room in an effort to locate the trouble. When he was brought back, the doctor assured me that he thought the hemorrhage was checked; nevertheless, he said he would stay the rest of the day to watch.

Parks had been stationed in Manila when the Japanese made their attack on Pearl Harbor, and he and the doctor discovered that they had many friends in common. It was good to see the aloofness disappear from the doctor's face as he and Parks talked, and I knew that I would never again feel that he was unfriendly. The doctor stayed with Hentz until five or six in the afternoon. I didn't know how to express my gratitude; he had been with him continually for more than thirty-six hours! I asked Parks to tell him. I knew he would know what to say.

After Hentz was given seven pints of blood, he felt fine again. It always astonished me to see how quickly he rallied after serious setbacks. He must have had an exceptionally strong constitution.

Everything went smoothly for a few days, until Hentz

began to suffer excruciating pain in the lower part of his abdomen. Doctors came and went all that day. Nothing they gave by hypodermic eased him, and in the afternoon the neurosurgeon did a spinal block. Still the pain continued. Unable to cope with anything more, I told my nephew, Bill Hentz, to go to the telephone and tell Fred that he must come. Tracy stayed at the hospital with us until Fred arrived at 11:00 P.M. He said he had jumped in the car, driven to Atlanta, and caught the first plane. When he was with us I'm afraid I let him have more than his half of the burdens —at least, mine seemed lighter by more than half.

Fred stayed on for several days, and Hentz still had no relief from the pain. At last Fred told us he would have to leave, and in my disturbed state of mind I couldn't imagine what could be important enough to make him go. Surely other things could wait. But by now both of us knew that we would go on, and that we knew where we could go for the strength to do so.

Fred and I were in the darkened ward with Hentz that last night of his stay in New York. Just before midnight he said, "I must go now." In the faint light from the hall I could see the tears in his eyes. He walked out of the quiet ward without looking back, and left us there to battle with the pain.

I've never felt more completely without resources than when Hentz looked at me with eyes tortured with pain and asked, "How could he leave?"

All I could say was: "I don't know. I don't know. I don't believe I know anything." But in a little while I felt the strength coming back and I knew that I *did* know one thing: somehow God would help us through the bad places.

After six hideous days Hentz was taken to the operating room, where a small stone was moved from the urinary tract.

The relief was instant. I think this puzzled the doctors, because Hentz was not supposed to feel anything at all below his chest. It also gave me something to build more hope on. Perhaps the main nerve was healing!

A day or two after Hentz was relieved of the pain, surgery on the kidney was performed. He rallied better than anyone thought he could. Fred didn't come for this operation because he had just left New York; but Parks, Lois, and Tracy were with me. The neurosurgeon saw us sitting in the hall by the elevator, waiting for Hentz's return from the operating room, and he stopped to talk a minute. He turned to me and said: "I hope you don't feel that you have been singled out to be made to suffer. Life for all quadriplegics is a series of complications. I wish I could paint a prettier picture for you, but I can't." He said that he wished he knew the condition of Hentz's spinal cord, but that he would never look at it because it was too dangerous. He said he knew the neurosurgeon from Atlanta had not looked at it because he had written and asked him.

The Miners' Ward had lost its strangeness. I was no longer persistently conscious that the patients were paralyzed: now they were personalities. We were among the initiated; and when a new patient was being admitted I knew how he felt, and wished I could do something to make the strangeness less noticeable. I was timid about speaking to the new ones, because I had discovered that many people who were not Southerners were suspicious of friendly overtures. Sometimes one of the other patients would call across the aisle to the newcomer, "Hard or soft coal?" and I wondered how he knew he was speaking to a miner, and why nobody had said "Hard or soft coal?" to us. The day that the miners' paper came—I think it was called the *United Mine Workers Journal*—was a big day. The man who passed them around always gave me a copy, and I thanked him graciously. I used to laugh and ask Hentz what he thought would happen to me if I said something, in a loud voice, derogatory to John L. Lewis. I had never formed a positive opinion about Mr. Lewis, but after seeing the respect and devotion of these miners I did form one—and it was in his favor.

The nurses and the patients told me that the United Mine Workers Fund paid a tremendous yearly sum to ensure the admittance of an injured miner. I asked Dr. Howard Rusk, Director of the Institute of Physical Medicine and Rehabilitation, about it, and he said that such was not the case. The United Mine Workers pay the costs of their patients' care at the University Hospital as do the insurance companies and social and welfare agencies. He said they had found it better to combine the patients in one ward who were in need of the type of surgery and medicine to be found at the hospital, as they are a help to one another, just as they combined them at the Institute.

I found that some of the men and boys who were patients in the ward were on my heart and mind no matter where I went. One whom they called Hutch was morose and moody. He had had several major operations, and the nurses said his mental attitude was very poor. Of course, I wanted to know why. His wife had deserted him when he broke his back, and no one cared whether he stayed for months in a New York hospital or not. He talked to no one, and would not look at television. He often asked for sedatives so that he could sleep the long hours away. It was a happy day for me when he asked me to do a favor for him. For a while he seemed much better, and began laughing and talking with the other patients. When the nurses brought his medication, he no longer said: "I don't want any of your medicine. Leave me alone!"

One night I stayed at the hospital late because Hentz was not doing well. The ward was dark, and I was sitting by Hentz's bed with the men and boys all around me. I felt strange and uncomfortable surrounded by the sleeping men, some snoring loudly, some gently. I wondered how they ever could find forgetfulness long enough to fall asleep. Suddenly I was conscious of a sound that definitely was not a snore. I listened closely, thinking I might hear it again. It happened again. Now I knew that it was a sob that had escaped from one of the occupants of the dismal room after a desperate effort to suppress it. There was another sob. I hadn't heard many men cry, and the sound was terrible. Which of these laughing, taunting, swearing men or boys was lying awake in the long dark room? I got up very quietly and tiptoed toward the sound. As I neared Hutch's bed, there was another terrible sob; the effort that was being made to stifle it only made it more racking. I stood by his bed and yearned to touch his head so that he would know there *was* someone who cared, but I was afraid. With a feeling of futility I returned to Hentz's bed. I never knew if Hutch knew that I stood by his bed. He could have seen my feet because he was lying face down, and there was a dim light from the hall. After that night he was more friendly and talked more freely.

These experiences affected me deeply; I could not forget them. The knowledge that I couldn't do anything to help made them so much worse for me. I had always run from sickness and accidents. All my life I couldn't bear to see anyone hurt. I remember once when I was a very young child a little friend broke his arm while we were playing baseball. When the little boy fell and cried, we gathered around him —then I saw his arm and the terrifying crookedness. I ran and ran and ran. I thought if I went far enough I could get away from his pain. And now I spent many hours each day in the midst of more pain and tragedy than I'd ever known existed. Men called me to their beds and showed me sores on their bodies that made me want to recoil in horror and run as I had when I was a child; but I stood quietly and assured them that plastic surgery would close the wounds. Sometimes I couldn't believe that these things actually happened—not to me. At times when I was away from the hospital, with friends, and I heard myself laugh, I would stop suddenly and wonder how I could possibly indulge in gaiety. I don't suppose you ever get used to this kind of suffering—you just get used to hiding how much it hurts you.

A young man in a bed across the aisle from Hentz made me wish I could write poetry. After the grief he had had to face in his short life, how could his face have that look of serenity and gentleness and youth? When I watched him moving with amazing speed through the ward on his crutches, smiling at everyone he met, I felt that lost kind of wonder I feel when I look upon something too mysteriously lovely for me to comprehend. I felt as I did when I watched a man seated near me at a concert in Carnegie Hall, and envied him because in my ignorance I could not experience whatever it was that caused the look of rapture on his face.

I learned many things while visiting in the Miners' Ward. From necessity I was close to the suffering that I had suspected was in all the world. Even though I had always run from pain and sickness, I learned to be stoical in situations that would have once caused me to cry out or escape.

I learned the meaning of courage. I learned the true meaning of bravery—it isn't being able to meet a big, sudden emergency. It is meeting the same ugly, crushing, relentless enemy every morning and smiling and pretending that the enemy is not there. In that dingy room I saw more beauty than in all my life before.

There is no beauty in bed sores and wasted and deformed limbs. But when a man smiles because the man in the bed next to him smiles; when a man is determined to have a good life in spite of great odds; when a man whispers words of comfort and hope to another man in pain; when a man knows that with God helping him he can taste the sweetness of victory—on such a man's face there is beauty.

After a while New York seemed smaller, and I came to know a little section that was almost as familiar to me as Perry. I no longer felt alien and out of place. Even though I didn't know the shopkeepers well enough to say "Good morning," as we do at home, I knew their faces, which were beginning to look like faces everywhere else.

I ate breakfast in a little place under the Third Avenue Elevated tracks that would be considered a "dump" in New York, Atlanta, or Perry—and I felt delightfully at home there! The waitresses called the old bums who ate there "honey" and "dearie," and the bums told their troubles while the waitresses murmured sympathetic and comforting words. I tried all the eating places in the vicinity of my hotel, but this place had by far the best breakfasts. Yet it wasn't the food alone that made me return. I went back day after day because of a particular waitress. If I missed a day she was worried—and the moment I walked in she asked me about Hentz. The first time I tried to get Fred to eat there with me he balked—he didn't like to sit on a stool—and he had many plausible reasons for not going. Finally he agreed to go just once. My favorite waitress called him "dearie," and I believe he liked it—especially when she asked him about Hentz. She had a son about Hentz's age who was a leader in school activities, and who had had many honors bestowed on him. When he was ready for college, she said, he could almost take his choice of scholarships. I liked to hear her talk about her son. Having my breakfasts in the little unstylish eating place started the day off on a happy note, and I wouldn't have traded it for the Waldorf! On one of Parks's visits he had lunch with me there, and I believe he was the first colonel to have done so. After his visit they treated me with more deference, which disappointed me.

During the latter part of March, 1952, while Hentz was still at the University Hospital, Leonora, Louise, and Felton Norwood drove to New York to see us. I think everyone in Perry sent Hentz a present, and it took several trips for the orderlies to bring all the packages into the hospital. There were fruit cakes, candies, cookies, books, flowers, magnolia leaves for me to put in the lobby of my hotel, late-blooming camellias, and early peach blossoms. There were also several pounds of Georgia barbecue packed in dry ice!

This was Felton's first trip to New York, and we had fun showing him the magic city. Because he was studying music, I took him to Carnegie Hall—and from there to the flea circus! It made me feel years younger to have them with me, and we went to my room to eat the wonderful foods Fred's mother prepared for them.

When the day came for them to go back to Georgia, I couldn't bear to see them leave. Lois Crews must have known how I felt about the Perry folks leaving, so she asked me to go with her to the International Flower Show, and to lunch with a friend of hers who is a television actress. Because it was raining, I took a taxi to the hospital to see how Hentz was—and pretended that I had come to get an umbrella I had left there. When I walked into the ward, I saw a woman doctor and Dr. Covalt by Hentz's bed.

I said: "Dr. Covalt, I didn't come visiting so early. I came for my umbrella."

He replied: "Come any time you want to. Please feel free to do so."

As I turned to leave I heard the woman doctor say, "Dr. Covalt, Hentz is about ready to go to the Institute." My spirits began to soar. No one had told me, and I didn't know, if any more operations had been planned. I suppose I had begun to think that Hentz would be in the hospital forever. The flowers at the show probably were not nearly so pretty as I thought they were!

I suppose in all large cities representatives of different religious sects visit hospitals in large numbers. Back home anyone who wasn't a Methodist, Baptist, or Presbyterian was the rare exception. In Macon the Protestant churches select a list of ministers to serve as visiting chaplain at the different hospitals for a period of one week; the young priest from the Catholic church visited twice a day. The visits from the Protestant chaplains were primarily of a friendly and social nature. Some of the ministers were friends of ours, or of our families. In New York our denominational visitors were definitely concerned with the state of the patient's soul, and at least one of them, a young man from New Jersey, spoke at great length about the necessity of joining his group or of being eternally lost. Hentz said some of the visitors and the colored man who was the night nurse had very animated discussions. He pretended that these talks left him with fantastic notions of salvation and the hereafter. Therefore I was glad, one morning, to open a letter from the Presbyterian minister in Perry with some unexciting Presbyterian literature enclosed. After hearing several other interpretations of the Bible, it seemed about as dull as *The Pilgrim's Progress* after reading a mystery thriller. Nevertheless it *was* comforting to read again about tranquillity, after tracts that told of the tortures waiting for us if we didn't repent and join the young man from New Jersey.

One day when I arrived at the hospital I found Hentz on the tilt board. In front of him was a tall table littered with writing paper, and he had a ballpoint pen strapped to his hand. He told me to look at the letter he had written to Fred. It was his first attempt at writing, and the letters were large and irregular. I couldn't say anything because of the lump in my throat. He said, "Well, I know it isn't good, but you needn't seem quite so unimpressed!"

Not impressed! I longed to put my arms around him as he stood there, looking so tall strapped to the board. The poor scrawl of that first letter to Fred was visible proof to me that God had given my son strength to overcome every obstacle.

CHAPTER TEN

On March 27, 1952, we reached another milestone. It was the day Hentz would finally be transferred to the Institute. We had yearned and prayed for this moment. Now it arrived.

As I reached the University Hospital, Hawkins the colored attendant was busy with the final details of packing. Hentz was dressed, sitting in the wheel chair and eager for the new adventure. John, the pleasant, gray-haired man who drove the Institute station wagon, came to tell Hawkins to roll Hentz out of the ward and to the waiting vehicle. Hentz was thrilled at the prospect.

Hawkins rolled Hentz in his chair up the ramp, and into the station wagon. I got in the front seat with John and a nurse who was attending little Alfredo, a polio case. I turned around and asked Hentz, "How are you doing? Can you see anything?"

He laughed half-heartedly, "Yes, I can see the tires on the automobiles."

It was our understanding that each room was to accommodate four patients with similar tastes and background. The first disappointment came when we realized that Hentz would temporarily have to share a room with an elderly man who was in great pain.

Before getting settled in his new quarters, Hentz asked to tour the building. We went up to the top floor to get a skyline view of the city. I could not help wondering how many of the city's millions suffered more than we can ever know. I felt terribly unimportant as I looked out the window. There was that old "what difference does it make?" attitude. I don't like to get that feeling of unimportance because, while it allays our wretchedness it also takes the glory out of overcoming. At the same time, the first impression of the old man in Hentz's room troubled me. My fears were confirmed; the next day my son was greatly upset. The elderly man had cried throughout the night. Hentz was rather discouraged by the incident and was ready to return to Perry. The only solution to this new turn of events was to request that Hentz be transferred to another room. Fortunately, the change was arranged.

Hentz was now located on the first floor, just above the ground floor, in an attractive room furnished with an adjustable bed, a chest of drawers, and a locker. Conveniently nearby were recreation rooms for all sorts of activities such as typing, watchmaking, musical studies, and so on. The therapy is called "Activities of Daily Living."

An atmosphere of hope and good cheer is sensed immediately upon entering the New York University-Bellevue Department of Physical Medicine and Rehabilitation, which is situated at Thirty-fourth Street between Roosevelt Drive and First Avenue. I was greatly impressed by its ultramodern architecture. The large reception room with its modern furniture, the immaculate marble walls and flooring, the high windows with rose-colored curtains, spelled a welcome in capital letters. The really memorable impression came from the large protrait of Dr. Simon Baruch, the father of Bernard Baruch. Their dreams can never die as long as hope shines on the face of each new patient.

A few nights after Hentz was moved to the Institute, I took him upstairs to see a movie at his insistence. When I learned that the picture was *The Men*, with Marlon Brando, I regretted his decision. I sat far back in one corner so as to appear detached and disinterested in Hentz. He saw the other patients rolling their chairs at frightening speeds, and I knew that he wished he didn't have to have so much help. When the picture began I felt shame for my own good health. The picture had been made at a rehabilitation center, and it was terribly painful for me to witness. Suddenly, as I sat there wishing the film would break, I heard laughter. They were laughing, and Hentz was laughing with them! Evidently the picture was already out of date, and rehabilitation methods had made great progress. At the time the picture was filmed, doctors and therapists hadn't conceived of making paraplegics walk. The best they had hoped for was a wheel chair. The patients, with their unbuckled leg braces and canes by their chairs, enjoyed the picture more than anyone else. However, they didn't laugh during the scene in which a grave doctor told a patient "not to expect miracles, because they just don't happen." I couldn't look at Hentz then. Suddenly I believed that man wants to believe more in miracles than in anything else in the world. When the picture was over, I didn't ask Hentz how he liked it. I hoped very much that it hadn't affected him as it had me. Much later I learned that none of the things that caused me such a sudden pang had the same effect on him. I wish I could have known earlier.

Several days after Hentz's arrival at the Institute he was notified that he would have to be evaluated. At that time the decision is made as to what can be done for the patient, how long it will take, and how it should be undertaken. Whenever it is decided that *nothing* can be done, the patient is sent home.

Nurses, doctors, physical therapists, and psychiatrists from all over the city gathered in the room where the movies were shown. Dr. Covalt had asked me to get Hentz and to wait with him in the hall outside the door. They discussed Hentz's case before he went in. Then someone came for him, and they looked at him and discussed him some more. I remained in the hall until Dr. Covalt sent for me. My heart was thumping, and my knees threatened to quit functioning. Suppose they told me that there was nothing they could do for Hentz?

They asked me a few questions, and were very considerate in every way. In a little while they said we could go, and I rolled Hentz out. I didn't see how I could wait until I heard the outcome of the evaluation.

A day or two after the evaluation Hentz had to see the psychiatrist for an interview. When we got back to his room he said the psychiatrist wanted to talk to me. I had never had any dealings with psychiatrists—except on a social basis. We knew a very delightful one during the depression who was doing general practice because back in the thirties people couldn't afford nervous breakdowns.

The New York psychiatrist quietly asked me to be *seated*. Perhaps part of their technique is to remain quiet and see what the patient will say—except that I didn't feel like a patient. I think that if I hadn't started talking, we would simply have sat there and stared at each other, so I talked about Hentz. He was very nice and allowed me to talk about him all I wanted to. I tried very hard to convince him that our relations were good and happy, and that it wasn't unhappiness at home that had made Hentz careless and resulted in his unfortunate dive. I had no way of knowing his reaction, because he sat with the same fixed smile throughout the monologue. When I could think of nothing more to say, and he said nothing either, I asked if I might go. Though he said he wanted to talk to me from time to time, he probably meant he wanted me to talk to *him* from time to time.

A day or two following our interview—or monologue—with the psychiatrist, Hentz was given an attendant of his own. Though we had not heard the result of the evaluation, my anxiety was eased because I knew he would not need an attendant if plans had not been made for him to stay.

The attendant was a colored man named Bill Pryor, and Hentz liked him immediately. Hentz always liked the colored employees because he understood them. With the employees from foreign lands, and even with New Yorkers, there was a gap that had to be bridged before their relationship was easy and natural—but not with the Negroes. Bill had lived in Virginia until he was twelve, when he moved to New York. He was thirty-two, married, and had five little girls. He was so full of good cheer and gaiety that he danced into the room every time he entered. When I asked him his name, he said, "Bill." He looked as though he had several hundred white teeth, because he laughed so much. As I talked to him I thought, How blessed we are that Bill laughs! Bill said that he would take Hentz to his classes, put him on the tilt board, and take him to the dining room, and that when there was nothing else to do they would see New York!

On the first Saturday afternoon that Hentz was at the Institute I hurried back from the Metropolitan Opera House, where I'd gone with two of Anne's friends to hear Kirsten Flagstad in *Alceste*. During the week I had gone to a library to borrow a libretto so that I could impress my new friends with my knowledge; but I had to laugh at myself when I discovered that the opera was being sung in English.

I had promised Hentz that I would take him to ride in a taxi, but some of the men who worked at the Institute said Hentz's chair would not go into a taxi. Because I could see his disappointment, I rolled his chair around two or three blocks; but there was nothing very interesting in the vicinity of the Institute. As I looked up Thirty-fourth Street I saw James and Tracy coming toward us. I told them about our disappointment.

James said: "Who needs a taxi? Let's go!" He grasped the handles on Hentz's chair and started up Thirty-fourth Street at a very rapid pace. Tracy said that James's father had been an invalid, and that James knew about wheel chairs. I could tell from the expert way he handled Hentz that he was no novice. James passed First Avenue, Second Avenue, Third Avenue, Lexington—and still he walked. Because I was tired, I suggested to Tracy that we get on a crosstown bus and not try to keep up with Hentz and James. We boarded a bus at the corner, and we went about the same speed as James. At times he would be ahead of us; then we would catch up and pass him.

Occasionally I could see Hentz laughing as he turned his head in every direction. I saw people quickly stepping out of the path of the fast-moving wheel chair. I admired the sureness with which James lowered the chair at the curbs and the way he tilted the chair back so that Hentz would not fall forward. Every now and then James would stop and point something out to Hentz, and lean close to him—probably to explain something, or to answer Hentz's question. Sometimes both of them would laugh at once.

James's hair was blown in the wind, but he didn't seem to mind. He didn't look like a young man who spoke five languages, knew music, art, books, antiques, could cook, paint a house or a picture, sew—just about everything. He was gay, and there was nothing about him that reminded me of some of the preachers I'd known. He found excitement in life, and gave excitement to it. I knew that when he had a church of his own he would make his listeners feel that they were missing a glorious adventure if they did not follow Christ. The way of life he'd recommend to them would be creative, joyful, one of love and peace.

The day was very cold, and I worried about Hentz having on proper clothing; but when I saw his shining face I knew that nothing so practical as warm clothes mattered. After eleven months he was out with well people again! I felt very grateful for friends like James and Tracy.

Hentz was in a room with people he liked, and his improvement was rapid. There seemed to be no limits to the tasks he assigned to himself, and I knew that nothing would stop him now. There were only three or four quadriplegics at the Institute, and I think all except one broke their necks diving. All of them had more muscular return in their arms than Hentz, as their breaks were lower down the spine. If use of the triceps and biceps both come back, the patient can roll his own chair. Hentz tried, and said he would do it.

One of the three other patients in Hentz's room was a man from Grand Rapids, Michigan. I suppose he was in his early thirties; he was married and had several children. He was very charming; and if he wasn't having the time of his life nobody would have ever suspected it. He had broken his back in an automobile accident, and his doctors had said he would be fortunate if he was ever able to sit in a wheel chair. Because he sold wood to the furniture factories in his city, he told his doctors: "I can't call on my customers in a wheel chair without an attendant. There are always steps."

The doctors said, "Well, you can go up the steps in a sitting position." But Dick was determined to find a more conventional way to carry on his activities.

After he went to New York to be rehabilitated, he must have set some kind of record. In no time he was walking with braces and canes; he learned to drive an automobile; he learned how to get in a tub; and he laughed all the time he learned. He could do uncanny things with his crutch; and sometimes, when he was reaching for an object high in his locker, he'd look at me and say, "I don't see how you poor old normal people manage without a crutch!" He learned so many things with such amazing speed that he was called upon to give demonstrations to visiting therapists and doctors.

One day he was called before one of the doctors, who said: "Dick, I simply cannot understand it. You are progressing so much faster than any of the other paraplegics. How do you do it?"

Dick said: "They are insurance cases, and I'm paying for this myself. I've *got* to learn fast!"

Another patient in the room was a delightful man from the Midwest and he was the pet of the Institute. I never knew what caused his disability, but one of the nurses said it was a brain injury. He spoke with great difficulty, and walked on crutches with very poor coordination; in fact, he stayed in the wheel chair except during practice periods. The orderlies said Joe was a millionaire; but I'd learned that anybody who didn't have a paper suitcase was a millionaire. He had taught at a college, and I didn't know many millionaires who were college professors. Joe's brother, who visited him often, was a doctor. He quit practicing for a while to write a book. He had written several, I believe, and the latest one was *No Place to Hide*. It was about the Hiroshima bombing. He and Joe enjoyed teasing Hentz about Southern politics— it was just prior to the Democratic convention in Chicago. Hentz presented a strong case for the Dixiecrats—and for Senator Russell for President.

The fourth person in the room was an elderly man who had been frozen in a milk refrigeration plant, and who had been completely paralyzed. He was beginning to regain the use of his limbs.

Hentz thought they had the nicest room in the Institute. It was gratifying to see him so happy.

Tracy asked me if I'd like to move to the apartment where she lived. The room was nice, large, and bright, so I was glad to go with her. There were two other women in the apartment, one who was retired, and one who worked on *Time* magazine. The apartment was very large, and all of us shared the kitchen and bath, which were immaculate. The retired maiden lady saw to it that we did everything according to her own rigid standards. Tracy and I had to rinse out all tin cans and milk cartons before putting them into the garbage cans. Though I ate only my breakfast in the apartment, I was supervised carefully. The retired lady told me that in the thirty-five years she had worked in a bank, she had never misfiled a single item! In the face of such perfection, I felt exceedingly negligent.

Tracy left the apartment early every morning to go to the library at Columbia to read. She was trying to get started on her thesis. I slept later than she did, and it was comforting to arise and find one of her little notes near the door. Just to know that somebody in New York cared enough to write a cheery message and slip it under your door was a big help.

Before long, the capable retired lady realized that I would cooperate with her in her relentless battle against roaches —although I hadn't seen one—and she offered to buy my groceries for me. She knew I liked to go to the Institute in time to do the little shopping the men had asked me to do. I began to like her, and tried not to notice when she complained that her income did not permit the luxuries she craved. I think I would have become discontented, too, if I had had to share my home for fifteen years with an endless stream of strangers who had to be taught to rinse out milk cartons!

During the Easter season Bill pushed Hentz all the way to the theater district to see *Three Wishes for Jamie*, and pushed him back again. Hentz had ordered another wheel chair, custom-made to fit his particular needs. When it came, he and Bill would be able to ride in taxis. I was at the Institute waiting for them to return from the show. I had been down on Fourth Avenue rummaging in the old bookstores, and I had bought a book for Fred called *The Confederate Side*, and two old books written by my great-grandmother.

When Bill rolled Hentz into the room, I saw an orchid

tucked into the strap on Hentz's hand. He raised his arm and said: "Here's something I brought to you. It's had a pretty rough time, but it looked all right when Bill and I started out with it." He laughed as I pulled the orchid tube out of the strap and looked at the bedraggled flower. It was limp, and frayed around the edges. Though the poor bloom had had to fight the hustling breezes off the rivers, and the hustling people on the avenues, that only made it more beautiful to me.

I tried to keep my gratitude on a light plane as I pinned the flower on my lapel. I said: "I shall always keep it. When it's completely wilted, I'll press it in a book as my father's family did with their flowers of sentiment. I'll put it in *The Confederate Side.*"

To this day the pale and colorless ghost of the flower my son brought me lies in the book together with the dead of the Confederate and Union armies.

None of the doctors said anything about Hentz not living —they were too busy making plans for his future. I was on the crosstown bus one day when an attractive young woman named Miss McCormick, who was in charge of the Activities of Daily Living at the Institute, sat by me. She was leaving the next day to visit several large cities to deliver addresses on the rehabilitation program. She worked with Hentz, and was highly pleased with his progress—and we were grateful to have her because she was one of the best. She said: "There is so much in store for Hentz, though it will be slow—very slow." We didn't mind now about the good things coming slowly; and how good it was to hear her words of hope and optimism! I think that we, the impatient, nervous ones, were learning patience. Fred had always possessed it, but Hentz and I were deficient in that admirable quality. But we could wait—as long as we could work and hope while we waited.

One Sunday afternoon friends of Lois' from Japan asked Lois and me to go to a Christian Science lecture at the Waldorf-Astoria Hotel. I was surprised at the large number of people and at the happy expressions on their faces. Later I told Hentz that they looked happier than any people I'd seen in New York except the ones at the International Flower Show. He said, "It looks as though you must be either a horticulturist or a Christian Scientist to look happy in New York."

Lois Crews was very wonderful to me, and I worried for fear she was neglecting some of her many duties to be with me. Whenever I was lonely, and Tracy was out, I wanted to call Lois and talk to her, but I didn't feel that I should. She was writing a book, writing radio scripts, doing P.T.A. work and social activities, and she had a child, a home, and a busy husband. I thought she was being nice to me because of her great affection for Anne Griffin. One day I telephoned to tell her that Hentz had told me that the feeling had spread down a little into the palm of his hand. I was so excited and pleased that I had to share the good news. Lois, who has a gift of making her pleasure, sympathy, and gaiety felt over the telephone, said: "Oh, Harriet, thank you for telling me! I surely must mean something to you for you to want to share this with me."

From that minute I knew Lois liked *me* for my own sake. I knew I'd found a friend that wouldn't be just a New York friend; she would be an all-time friend. Though she never tried to minimize our troubles, she did magnify our ability to carry on. She never said, "You know, you can always find

someone else worse off than you are." So many people said
that, thinking they'd hit on the magic formula that would
bring comfort. How could anyone be made happier knowing
that a fellow man was having a rougher time of it?

During one of Fred's visits to New York James and Tracy
came to the Institute. James said Bill Webber, dean of stu-
dents of Union Theological Seminary, had loaned him his
carry-all in order that Hentz might tour the city. James had
taken the seats out of the back hoping that Hentz's chair
could be rolled inside. The chair was too tall, so Hentz sat in
the front with James and Fred. Bill Pryor, Tracy and I sat
on the floor in the back. After a long ride during Manhattan's
late afternoon rush hour we took Bill home, then decided
to go some place for dinner. Hentz couldn't get out of the
carry-all, so Fred and James said they would think of something. They parked in front of a nice looking Italian restau-
rant on a good street and they went inside. In a few minutes
a very proper looking man in a tuxedo stepped to the window
of the carry-all and said, "I will take your orders for dinner,
please." We gave him our orders. It took the waiter several
trips to get into the spirit of the thing, but after a while he
was laughing with us. He said, "We have never done anything like this before." James and Fred ate inside—the bums!
I know they didn't have as much fun as we did. Later, I had
dinner with James at Union Theological Seminary and I met
Mr. Webber. He said the carry-all was at James's disposal
any time that Hentz could go for a ride.

As Hentz improved, and learned to do many things for
himself, I stayed away from him more and more. I knew he
was too polite to enter into the activities at the Institute and

leave me. I talked to one of Hentz's doctors, who said he thought it would be better if I saw less of Hentz, because patients need to feel that they are independent. Hentz's general condition had improved considerably, and he didn't really need me.

Something Bill Pryor said made me think that Hentz might prefer to be in New York alone, so I began to think about going home. It was the last thing I really wanted, but I would do it if it would help Hentz to gain a new sense of self-confidence. For over a year he had been the center of all our thoughts and activities. I knew that then he wanted and needed us. Hentz had felt free to ask favors of me that he would not ask other people. When he felt well we had fun together, and he could say things to me that he wouldn't say to others. Though I knew in my heart that there was an understanding and a relationship between us that was good and right, I sensed that he didn't want the people at the Institute to think that he needed anything that couldn't be supplied there. It was time for Mother to go. My visits were beginning to embarrass him. It had nothing to do with his feelings for me, but much to do with his growing independence. I was a mother who was glad to see my son develop the thing he needed so much—and who was grief-stricken that that development naturally excluded me.

Lois and Tracy did everything they could to help during the days I was making the decision to go back to Perry. Lois would come in from her home in Port Washington and have lunch with me. Tracy also knew what a bad time I was having, and, in her quiet, gentle way, tried to divert me.

On one of the last days I was in New York, Hentz was standing up on the tilt board when I visited him. He had been reading, and there were magazines and letters on the high table in front of him. His arms were propped on the table. I was standing close to him, reading a letter on the table. Suddenly, without any warning, he raised his arms, put them around my neck, and said, "You're a nice old girl." It was the first time in a year that I had felt his arms around me.

Hentz was made one of the editors of the paper published by the patients at the Institute. One night the Recreational Director, Jack Ginsburg, was in Hentz's room, and said: "Don't forget to attend the newspaper writers' meeting on Monday night. You have the lead article, you know." I knew how it must please Hentz to be *doing* something again. I heard him tell someone at the Institute that he missed doing organization work very much. Before he was hurt he had rushed from one thing to another, and I had marveled at his activity.

On one of my visits I could tell that Hentz was worried about something, and after a while he began to talk. He said: "I talked with the vocational therapist today, and he asked me what I wanted to do when I got out of the hospital. I said I wanted to go to college. He told me that I might as well accept the fact that I would be dependent on my parents for a long time. That like to have killed me. It's very hard for me to think of my continuing dependence on you and Pop."

I wanted to put my arms around him, and tell him that it would be a joy for us to be able, always, to do for him. Instead I said: "All right, then. If you feel that way, write a book."

Hentz answered, "I've started one."

I didn't ask any questions, but I hoped he would tell me more about it. I wrote some things on a piece of paper that

Anne tells her pupils about writing: "What was your reaction to the situation? How did a thing smell? How did it feel? How did it look?" He smiled when he read what I had written. He said it *might* be helpful, and started sniffing in the air, and saying, "How did it smell?" He has inherited an uncanny sense of smell from me, and our noses have borne the brunt of many jokes. I reminded him that he couldn't write an entire book on how everything smelled!

When I put on my coat to leave, he told me to get the little note on the table he had written to me. He said it was the first time he had tried writing on the typewriter.
It read:

"Dear Hattie, Considering the great distance????separating us, this letter may arrive a few days late, but I wanted to wish you a happy Easter, and thank you and Pop for showing me such a good time over the holidays. Thanks also for the nice clothes you bought me.

"There is not much I can tell you that you don't already know, except this—when I seem to be disgusted with you, I am really disgusted with old me because there is so much I can't do for myself yet—so try to bear with me.

"This letter might not be the longest in the world, but this is my third day on it,—Love, Hentz."

As I walked out the front door that night, to get a bus to the air terminal, I left all but the functional part of my heart behind.

CHAPTER ELEVEN

Fred met me at the airport in Atlanta. The plane was several hours late because of motor trouble. It was good to see him, and we laughed a lot and he told me all the Perry news. I wondered what he had done to the house while I was away. He always did something to surprise me. It was pleasant riding in the night, and I was relieved to know that I could feel carefree so far from Hentz. Things were going better than I had thought they would.

When we got home the sky was just beginning its change from darkness to the first faint light, and the house and grounds looked pallid and completely lacking in character and warmth. I felt very detached and impersonal as I looked on this house that had been home. Not until I went inside did the realization strike me. It was the first time since Hentz had been hurt that we'd been home without him. I thought of something Anne had said: "When I'm with Hentz, I can't think that he is so handicapped. It's when I'm away that the enormity of it hits me." When I could see him, and hear him laugh and tease and plan, things seemed all right. But not now.

Not even Fred's surprise—the renovated bathroom upstairs —made me forget. Nevertheless, I tried to show the appreciation I felt.

I wished I could sleep for several months and not leave my room. I wanted to hide and lock the doors and not see anyone. It wasn't because I didn't need my friends; but I suppose I needed the solitude more. I think I made a good beginning toward becoming a tiresome neurotic. Fortunately, I recognized the fact. When I was invited to a big party friends of mine were giving at their lodge several miles from town, I accepted. There would be people from towns all around Perry, and I wanted to see them. Our friends throughout the entire section had been wonderful to us, and I wanted to thank them personally.

When I walked into the huge room filled with laughing, happy women, and they saw me, their kindness swept toward me like a wave. I could feel it; I felt caught up in it. They took my hands and wanted to know *all* about Hentz. They were so pleased that he was well enough for me to come home and get the rest they knew I must need. They didn't know that rest was not what I needed. They didn't know that I needed to see Hentz and let his grin soothe away my terrible fears. Suddenly I knew I couldn't stand it, and in desperation I sought out a close friend and asked her to take me home. I ran from kindness. I loved my friends, and I wanted to stay and tell them the wonderful things Hentz was doing, but I couldn't speak. I would die before I let them see me cry! So I ran.

Running home was cowardly, but it helped me to see things clearly again. We had to live our lives: God expected us to live them well; other people expected us to live them well.

After several hours alone in my room, I emerged knowing that I could do better. I expected temporary setbacks, but I wouldn't let them make me a recluse.

Hentz began writing letters to Fred and me, and the days on which we received one were glad days. The happiest day of the week was Sunday, because on that day he called us on the telephone. He sounded strong, and he could not have feigned the happiness that was in his voice. The reassurance the talks gave me lasted *nearly* until the next Sunday.

The telephone conversations and letters helped to ease the little stabbing hurts that were waiting for me every time I opened a closet, every time I went into Hentz's old room or looked at the electric train that I had saved for his children. In the closets, on a shelf or on the floor, I saw a steel back brace he'd used in the hospital next to a set of golf clubs; the sack of buckshot Margery had put on the end of a pulley for Hentz to pull and strengthen his arms lying near the springs and hand exercisers Hentz had ordered through an advertisement on the back of *Popular Mechanics* when he was a little boy.

On the morning of May 19, 1952, I waked with that depressing lethargy that anniversaries sometimes create. I didn't say anything to Fred about the date. If he'd forgotten I was glad he could. Every letter we received from Hentz told us more of the wonders that Miss McCormick was working with him in her class of Activities of Daily Living. On this day I decided to send him some kind of telegram to let him know that we had not forgotten the date. Because I knew he wouldn't want a sweet one, I wired: "Recent research reveals that one of the King's *Women* did rehabilitate Humpty Dumpty. Love, Mother."

Before many hours passed I received the answer: "Humpty loves Mother and Father Dumpty. That's no yolk. Humpty."

I felt great pride in my son. He wasn't up there brooding because a year ago every plan and every dream had vanished with that plunge in the lake. No, he was thinking up silly telegrams. I was thankful—deeply so.

Bill Pryor wrote long letters telling in detail the many things Hentz was doing. There were trips to West Point, demonstrations for visiting therapists, shows, circuses. He told us everything he knew we would like to know. We couldn't have possibly found anyone more suited to be Hentz's attendant.

Bill wrote about putting the Russell for President stickers that Fred sent on the windowpanes. He said that they had a Confederate flag on the television antenna, and that it blew proudly when the windows were opened. "Everybody is calling me a rebel now," he wrote. In every letter he told us of his respect and affection for Hentz, and said we had a son we could be proud of. He told us that he was going to write a book some day of all the funny things Hentz said.

In the middle of June, Fred and I asked Anne Griffin and Charles Bledsoe to accompany us to New York. New York had always had a fascination for me, but never before had I looked forward to a visit as eagerly as I did to this one. I thought the day of departure would never arrive. Anne no longer lived in Macon. She had accepted a position in a college in South Carolina. We wired her that we would pick her up in Columbia at 9:00 A.M.—and we were only *one* minute late. Fred, Charles, and I had left Perry at four. When the sun came out, the heat was oppressive, and traveling in the heat usually ruins my disposition; but nothing could shake my high spirits on this trip. Any old thing suited any of us, and we were very silly. Anne and Fred are usually sweet—but with Charles and me the sweetness is not a permanent thing. But on this trip politeness, consideration, fun, and excitement were everywhere. Charles had never seen New York, and I couldn't wait to show him the city. I knew he would like the places I liked. Showing a good friend New York is like sharing a good book: it makes for closeness and understanding. I knew he wouldn't care for the New York that tourists see. Anne liked the things we liked too, and we planned strange-sounding jaunts to auctions of antiques, and to shops that sell old copper and brass. Underneath all the plans and talk was the excitement of going to see Hentz. Everything funny seemed funnier as we visualized the joy it would be to tell Hentz. And once I thought I didn't want children!

We drove as if we were trying to establish some kind of record, and spent the first night on the south side of Baltimore in a lovely new motel. Fred and Charles had a room, and Anne and I stayed together. They thought we would call them the next morning and we thought they would call us; consequently, we slept until 10:00 A.M.! And after hurrying like sandpipers running from a beach ball! It didn't matter, though, because visiting hours at the Institute don't begin until 4:00 P.M. and we would get there in time.

Fred, Anne, Charles, and I walked into Hentz's room. He was in bed, and for a minute I was afraid he was sick. I kissed him on the forehead, and didn't think he would mind this show of affection in front of the other patients in the room. We all talked at one time, and told him about our trip. Hentz seemed aloof, and I thought that perhaps he felt a little embarrassed, as you sometimes do even with those closest to you.

I said: "Hentz, now that you are well enough to go places, we've planned a full schedule! Anne knows of a lot of restaurants that she wants us to try, and we want to take you to several shows. And did you know that I've never seen the Statue of Liberty?"

Hentz's smile was weak, and I felt a little hurt.

Fred said: "We brought you a bushel of the finest peaches you ever saw! Do you want me to get them?" Hentz said it would be a good idea, and dividing the peaches with the patients got us through the next few minutes. When that was done we all felt constrained again.

After a while I said: "Now you tell us what *you* want to do, Hentz. Maybe you have some better ideas about how we should spend our time in New York."

Charles said, "You know, Heinie"—one of our nicknames for Hentz—"that I'm counting on you to be my guide."

Surely Charles could make Hentz respond. But Hentz just smiled that weak smile again, and I felt my embarrassment and constraint turn to fear. Perhaps Hentz had been told something about his condition that we didn't know. We all became quiet.

Hentz was looking at the ceiling, and at last he said: "I can't go any place with you. I can't even get out of bed. My trip to West Point made a pressure sore on my sitting-down place, and I haven't sat up for three weeks."

I felt a mixture of relief and sympathy.

My Sister, and her husband, Wesley Bolin who is the Secretary of State of Arizona, and two of their boys, Bill and Wesley, were in New York at the same time as we. They were on their way to New Hampshire to a convention of the Secretaries of States. Seeing them made this trip to New York even more wonderful. Sister saw Hentz for the first time since he had been hurt. When she visited in Macon when Hentz was first hurt she would not go in his room. There were two reasons why she didn't see Hentz then. We feared that he would suspect that he was in a critical condition if so many of the relatives visited. Then too, she wanted to keep strong because I needed her so terribly, and she thought that seeing him would make her break down.

Mr. and Mrs. Van Diviere and their son Charles were in New York too. They had come with Charles to have his yearly evaluation. All of us stayed at the same hotel and visited and ate together.

While we were on this visit Hentz began to receive mail from Cincinnati, Ohio, and Denver, Colorado, and smaller towns in the vicinity of those two cities. We couldn't understand it. Some of the first letters upset Hentz somewhat because there was such an air of mystery about them. One envelope contained photographs of men's shoes—no word, just some very nice photographs of shoes. Another one had pictures of empty boxcars. At first we thought they were the work of a crank, and Fred suggested that Hentz not look at any more of them. With each mail the letters increased, until Bill had to make several trips to bring all of them to Hentz's room! It was unfortunate that the queer ones had to be first, because the ones that came later were eloquent proof of strangers' concern for a boy they thought they could help. After we left the Institute, the letters kept coming, and after Hentz returned to Perry they continued to come. There are literally hundreds and hundreds of them. Some neighborhood children counted them, and there were over nine hundred. The bulk of them came from the Cincinnati area.

For a long time we were simply at a loss to explain it, but before long one of the correspondents enclosed a small clipping that had been in the *Cincinnati Post,* and someone else sent the same story clipped from the Denver *Rocky Mountain News.* In a syndicated column someone—we don't know who it was—had written about Hentz. The little article told about him being at the Institute in New York, depressed because the doctors had told him that there was not much hope for his improvement. I don't really believe the doctors told Hentz anything like that, and I'm sure that if they did it would be difficult to learn that he was depressed. At any rate, the article was kind and the motive sincere. I can't imagine such a story moving that number of people to write, but it did.

There were so many of the letters that it took hours each day to read all of them, but it was fun. It was one of the most amazing evidences of the widespread belief in God's greatness and goodness that I've ever seen. They were filled with hope. They were cheerful. They told of obstacles that the writer had overcome by admitting God's power. Some were from people who wrote poorly, and some from people who were eloquent. In every letter, with the exception of the first ones with the unusual photographs, there was apparent the great desire to help a boy through a difficult time.

Because it was out of the question to answer all the letters, I wrote a letter to the editor of the *Cincinnati Post* asking him to thank the kind people there for us. He turned the letter over to a young lady who worked with the paper, and she wrote an article, using a picture of Hentz. I also

wrote to the editor of the *Rocky Mountain News* requesting
that he thank the people in that vicinity.

Several of the ones who wrote at first kept writing. A girl
in Loveland, Colorado, has been writing ever since. A couple
in Cincinnati still write; and they, with their mother, even
stopped to see us on their way to Florida. They were just
as precious as we thought from their letters that they would
be. Many people sent gifts of books and shirts and games.

If we had been cynics at the beginning of this experience,
the weight of the evidence of man's concern for his fellow
man would have altered our thinking.

The day came when we had to tell Hentz goodbye, but
it wasn't as difficult as it had been the first time. Now I
knew that he was better, and that the pressure sore was
only a temporary misfortune. He had told us that he could
feed himself; he could roll his wheel chair a little; he could
shave himself and brush his teeth. He could use the typewriter with an appliance strapped to his hands, and his
handwriting was improving. He was on the Recreation and
Patient Council, and he and one of his roommates were co-
editors of the patients' newspaper. He liked Bill Pryor, and
the doctors and therapists and the other patients, but best
of all, he was planning a full life for himself. He was planning
a life so full that there would be no time for self-pity and
regret.

As I walked out the door of the Institute this time, I was
not alone. Fred was with me. It wasn't dark, and I could
honestly believe that better days were *right* around the
corner. I knew that when I returned home this time I wouldn't
be haunted by objects in closets and in the attic. I was glad
that we had prayed and fought and believed.

CHAPTER TWELVE

The letters from Hentz began to have a homesick tinge to them, and when August came he wrote that he was seriously considering leaving New York. He believed that he could keep on with the exercises and other therapy at home. His desire to come home was a heartening sign to me. So many of the patients had a dread of leaving the protection of the Institute. Everything there was designed to their special needs, while the rest of the world seemed reserved only to those who were able-bodied. His letters told me that he was ready to tackle life, and I knew he felt enthusiasm for whatever was ahead. There was no hint of self-pity, bitterness, or remorse because of his radically altered life; there was only eagerness to get on with it. He wanted to get home in time to enter Mercer University, in Macon, in the fall.

Hentz wired to us that he and one of the therapists at the Institute, Lottie Ehrlacher, from Vienna, Austria, would arrive by plane in Atlanta on August 8, 1952. This news caused a happy upheaval, and we made preparations for another homecoming. Charles and I repainted the dining room which would now be Hentz's room. We papered one wall, between much laughing and splashing of paste, and matched the pattern in the paper beautifully. We were proud when people praised our professional-looking job.

The great day came, and there were the usual profusion of flowers and food, and more than the usual excitement. This time there would not only be Hentz, but also the strange young woman from Austria, who would be with us for two weeks. She was going to show us how to do things for Hentz with ease, such as getting in and out of the bed, in and out of the car, and getting dressed and taking the exercises.

Fred met Hentz and Lottie in Atlanta, and didn't get back to Perry until 10:00 P.M. There were about twenty-five relatives at the house when the car came in the drive-way. Many of us rushed outdoors to welcome Hentz home, and I think Lottie thought everyone was a little crazy. She looked on with a remote kind of surprise. Even before I spoke to Hentz, I wondered what we would do with Lottie for two weeks if she remained as aloof as she seemed.

Lottie opened the back door of the car, and I saw Hentz reclining on the seat on pillows. I felt embarrassed and unnecessary because of Lottie's air of complete capability. I could see that Hentz and Lottie had some kind of understanding about his problems that excluded us, and we all stood about looking foolish and eager to help. Lottie showed Fred and another man how to get Hentz out of the car. It looked quite easy. Fred rolled the chair to the house, and into the living room, where there were more relatives. In a low voice, and with a charming accent, Lottie said, "You can't sit up much longer." She and Hentz knew so much that we hadn't learned, and would have to learn. All of us felt clumsy in the face of their friendly, professional relationship.

I offered the guests refreshments, but no one wanted any. I thought it might make the situation a little more natural, but the relatives preferred to talk to Hentz and his attractive companion. I don't remember ever having felt so ill at ease with Hentz before, but I suppose it was my eagerness to have his home match the Institute in every comfort. I wanted Lottie to think we were the kind of parents who would help Hentz meet his problems, even though she had an air of mistrust.

As so often happens to people with different backgrounds, I was wrong about Lottie. The next day she seemed more friendly; the day following she was still more friendly; and in a few more days we discovered that she was a real comedienne. She was very dignified when we had company, but perfectly uninhibited with Hentz, Charles, Felton, and me; and we provided her with an appreciative audience. She was intelligent and knew her job, and quietly set about imparting some of her knowledge to us. Her father is an eminent orthopedic surgeon in Vienna, and some of the doctors from the Institute had met Lottie there while conferring with her father. She loved America, and especially so because her part of Vienna was occupied by the Russians.

She was conscious of our determination to do everything in our power to enable Hentz to have a good life. One day she cried with me about Hentz's courage, and the great and cheerful effort he was making to try to forget the limitations the accident had created.

Lottie saw at firsthand the eagerness of the people in Perry to help us. The weather was horrible, as August can be, and I didn't have trained help in the kitchen. When Hentz was hurt I'd let my cook go because we were not at home. I had a young girl to help with the cleaning, but she didn't come on Sunday. The first Sunday Lottie was with us was so humid and sticky that you could hardly breathe if you left the *one* air-conditioned room we had. A colored woman we called Aunt Celie had told me that she and another woman were going to do everything that had to be done that day. Aunt Celie had cooked for Fred's mother when he was a little boy, and we had a very real affection for her. The other woman said that Fred had helped her and her husband to buy their little home, and that she wanted to do something to show their appreciation. Before we finished breakfast, Aunt Celie and Aunt Beulah arrived dressed in snowy starched uniforms. Aunt Beulah said that she would do the cleaning and Aunt Celie the cooking. Aunt Celie was the best cook in our part of the country. Cooking for over a hundred persons didn't bother her, and she could broil chickens, make rolls and lemon tarts and sweet-potato soufflé and many other things with calmness and perfect assurance.

When our dinner was finished, and the house and kitchen were shining, I knew I could never have got through that August day without their help. I went to the kitchen to pay Aunt Celie and Aunt Beulah. I've never seen faces more surprised and hurt. I said: "But, Aunt Celie, Sunday is your big meeting day, and I want to give you something for being so wonderful to us. I can't accept such kindness."

She replied: "Please Ma'am, it makes me happy. I remember when my husban' was real sick, and you brought him your good electric fan. You forgot that? Not me! And that radio you lent him, and him blind and needing it so for company. No Ma'am, I still remembers. I loves all of you, and I trusts Mr. Houser more than any white man I know." Aunt Beulah was as firm in her refusal to accept pay for her work.

I was glad that Lottie was in Perry during the latter part of the peach season, for she was ecstatic over the tree-ripened fruit that people brought to us. The best peaches are the ones that don't ship well, and that is the kind that we received. Later, she told me that never again could she be happy with the peaches she could buy in New York.

Before Lottie's two weeks were up, we knew how to do things for Hentz, and do them with ease. She had an extension made over his bed, and Hentz could help swing himself out of his chair and into the bed with the aid of one person where formerly five were required. With the help of a heavy strap over the front door of the car, one person could swing Hentz from his chair into the car. These things meant the difference between having to stay at home most of the time and going about almost at will. Hentz could brush his teeth, shave, feed himself, and turn the pages of a book. When he demonstrated his accomplishments, and heard our surprised exclamations of wonder and pleasure, he said, "I'm rehabilitated!" Perhaps at one time I had thought rehabilitation meant more than this; but my gratitude was deep for the things Hentz could do, and the joy that doing them brought to him.

When Lottie went back to New York, we began living together again in the house as a family. There was no immediate prospect of returning to a hospital. All of us were eager to behave like normal people, and gradually we began to feel that we were.

At the suggestion of the doctors in New York, we had sent a colored boy from Macon to New York to learn how to care for Hentz. He stayed there a week, with Bill showing him the things that had to be done. It was obvious, the first day or two on the job, that he was too fond of intoxicating spirits. He lasted about two weeks. We were afraid he would hurt Hentz, and one Sunday, when he came to the house very drunk, we told him not to come back.

A boy from Perry had previously applied for the job, but we had been told that he wouldn't be satisfactory. He worked for a while in a home for elderly people, and the proprietor said he had "carried on too much foolishness." Because we desperately needed someone, I decided to learn more about the boy. After all, a little foolishness was harmless. A colored schoolteacher who knew him well told me that she thought we would like him. He had had a hard life and had to shift for himself. His mother died a few weeks after his birth, leaving him an orphan. He told me later that he had worked for his living since he was seven years old—which may or may not have been true, because Willie James would sacrifice truth for color any time.

I interviewed him, and later in the evening he came to the house to talk to Hentz. He was exceedingly talkative, and remained so the entire time he worked for us; but his cleanliness was another matter. Once, when I remonstrated with him about his personal cleanliness, he said, "Well, Mrs. Houser, I jus' natchully likes to be nasty"!

He was the strongest person I have ever known, and possessed the most amazing energy—accompanied by an unbelievable appetite. He ate more than any person I've ever known, but he rewarded us with the benefits of his energy.

One day, in the newspaper, we saw a news story about a kidney being successfully transplanted from one person to another. We teased Willie James, and told him that we were going to take one of his kidneys and transplant it in Hentz. He said, "I'd do anything for Hentz, but I don' think I can give up one of my kidneys."

One morning I came downstairs, and sat in the dining

room to drink a cup of coffee, and to read the morning paper. Willie James was in the kitchen working with such intensity that it wearied me to watch him. He had scrubbed the floor, and was scrubbing woodwork.

He said, "I'm bein' real smart so I can get off to go see a dead friend who gon' be on display at ten o'clock."

I said, "You certainly are full of vitality, Willie James. I'd give anything if I had your energy."

Hentz overheard us from his room, and called out, "*I'd give anything if I had his kidneys!*"

Hentz entered Mercer in the fall of 1952. He and Willie James left the house at nine for a ten o'clock class. It was hectic getting them off, because there was much to do, but I don't think they were ever late. At school there were many steps to be climbed, and we thought they would be an almost impossible hazard. Though there are sixty-five in one place they had to go, Willie could run up them, with Hentz in the wheel chair, with the agility of a squirrel. He was proud of the speed and the sureness of these daily ascents and descents, and he wanted to go to New York to establish some kind of record by taking Hentz to the top of the Empire State Building by way of the stairs! I think he could have done it.

Hentz was happy to be going to school. At last he was doing something constructive—and not just waiting for such a time to come. He would come back to Perry after his classes and rest a while, and on many nights he returned to Macon for meetings, parties, and dinners. When he came home from these affairs he would have to study, and to expedite matters I wrote his homework. He could have done it, but not when in bed, and when he came in from other activities he had to go to bed. I especially disliked doing the Spanish, and many mornings I had to get up earlier to rewrite the lesson because in the night Hentz had decided that we should have "soy" where we had "estoy."

Hentz insisted upon taking his examinations with the rest of the class, without being shown special consideration. Each day I could see his determination to be treated like other people grow stronger and stronger, but his writing must have given the professors a bad time.

When Hentz first started to school, I went to Macon with him and Willie James every morning and stayed at a friend's house until it was time to meet them and go home. Willie James was a show-off when he was driving, and we didn't feel easy when he and Hentz went alone. After a while I saw that Hentz resented being treated as a child; he said it lessened his feeling of independence for me to go with them. So I stopped going, after pleading with Hentz to try to keep Willie under control, and after asking God *please* to take care of them.

Every day Hentz said or did something that caused me to offer up a prayer of gratitude. He evinced a good-humored acceptance and willingness to meet the challenges that were constantly before him. When he joked about himself at first, I was shocked; then I discovered that I could joke too! One day he came home from Mercer and announced that he was going back that night to a dance. While I was wondering how he could bring himself to go to a dance, he said, "Of course, I don't dance very well, but I won't let that keep me home."

Hentz was pledged to Kappa Alpha fraternity, and I think Fred was disappointed that he did not accept the bid to the one to which he belonged. Because Hentz had a urinary infection the night the pledges turned in their decisions, he couldn't go back to Macon. He asked me to roll him to the telephone, and he called the fraternity house of his choice and told them of his decision. I could hear the whooping and yelling as I stood nearby. The boys knew how awfully disappointed he was that he couldn't be in Macon for the pledging ceremony; and in about forty-five minutes, when I answered a knock on the door, there stood a crowd of boys and girls. They said, "Mrs. Houser, we came to pin Hentz's pledge pin on him." How wonderful for them to do such a thing! I asked them into the living room, and Fred rolled Hentz in. I fought with a troublesome lump in my throat as one of the boys put the pin on Hentz's chest. They made all of us feel that having Hentz was a privilege for them— and I thought they were the finest young people I ever saw. Fred was completely won over by them, and said later that he couldn't feel any regret about Hentz's choice after seeing the kindness of the Kappa Alphas.

The boys at the fraternity house asked Willie James to be their butler. Willie thought he was one of the brothers too. At one of the meetings Hentz was informed that he had to do thirty hours' work for the chapter, such as polishing brass and cleaning the suite. Willie James offered to do Hentz's chores, but Hentz refused. He said he would do his own work, and offered to do any typing they needed done. Hentz had us make a mitten of lamb's wool and tie it to his hand, and he polished brass and shoes with it.

One day when Hentz and Willie James came in from school I could see that Hentz was unusually happy. He cocked his head and said, "Hattie, you are now looking at the president of the K.A. pledge class." As he spoke, I saw how much the honor meant to him. Suddenly I felt such a surge of gratitude for the boys at school that I almost told Hentz how much I loved them. And I did love them!

Hentz did good work at school, and if he came home with a B plus Fred and I reminded him that that wasn't good enough. We expected as much from him as we ever had. To us he could admit that he hadn't quite finished answering all the questions on the examination, but he wouldn't tell anyone else that. He had to write so slowly that I never understood how he could answer half the questions.

Activities at the school and the fraternity gave Hentz something to do and think about. He was on committees to make floats for parades; and his enthusiasm for some of these activities exceeded mine, because I was pressed into making many objects that were definitely out of my line.

Willie James's exuberance and wild imagination were real problems. He tried my patience to such a point that I was extremely nervous, and trembled at times as though I were palsied. It was frustrating to be so dependent upon him, and to know that I would have to tolerate his foolishness because Hentz needed him. Fred kept telling me not to say anything to Willie because of our desperate need. I thought a very plain talk would help, but Fred discouraged me, so I boiled and boiled. One day Willie left Hentz at the fraternity house in Macon and took our car and courted a Negro girl for two hours—while Hentz waited and the brothers looked for Willie. Hentz was furious when they got home, and he read the riot act to Willie because his rendezvous had caused Hentz to sit up much too long. After that Willie was a changed young man. I marveled, and hoped the change would be permanent.

I talked to Willie about his shortcomings; but, though he graciously acknowledged them with fervent promises to do better, the promises were always soon forgotten. We couldn't think of letting him go, because of the expert way he handled Hentz, managing the wheel chair as though he had done it all his life. He thought nothing of scooting up the stairs at our house—and they are difficult ones. He could swing Hentz from the chair into the car as effortlessly as if Hentz were weightless.

Everything Willie did was for effect. When guests knocked on the door, Willie put on a performance of Southern hospitality, graciousness, and consideration for their comfort that charmed every caller. I could hear him imitating someone in the Movies or TV: "Won't you *please* come in? Mrs. Houser is upstairs, and I'll call her." In the summertime he'd say: "Can I get an ilectric fan for you? Or would you like a Coca-Cola or a glass of water?" In the wintertime he was concerned about the temperature of the room. Greeting strangers was the thing he loved most, and he always managed to be the center of attention, one way or another. When he was raking leaves in the yard, and there was no visible audience, he would sing so loudly that everyone in the neighborhood could hear him. He mowed and raked the yards with unbelievable speed because people passing remarked on how rapidly he worked, and compared him enviously with workers they had. This pleased him, and he ran the power mower so fast he nearly shook it to pieces. When he drove the car, he steered with one finger when we reached Macon or downtown Perry. I suppose he enjoyed living more than anyone else because he never ceased to perform before an appreciative, if imaginery, audience.

Willie James learned to use the tools Hentz had before he was hurt. He executed Hentz's designs for gadgets and appliances to make life less complicated. Both of them

seemed happy when they were making these gadgets. Hentz
would tell Willie exactly where to bore every hole and where
to put every screw. I used to marvel at the calm and unresent-
ful way in which he watched Willie work. I knew that Hentz
knew that if he could use his hands he would execute his
plans more skillfully than Willie could, but his patience was
a miracle. One day they made a little gadget, which we
call a "picker-upper," that revolutionized Hentz's life. Fred
wanted to play chess with Hentz; the young people wanted
to play Scrabble and bridge; boiled peanuts had to be picked
up, or else someone would have to do it for him; screws
had to be chosen for the work he and Willie did. All one
day Hentz and Willie worked. At one time they asked me if
they could break up an aluminum chair on the screened
porch. I said that if the cause was worth while they could
demolish the chair. I would not refuse Hentz anything that
helped him to satisfy his creativeness. He and Willie got
leather, fishing lines, and opened drawers and emptied their
contents until the house was a mess.

A few days after the "picker-upper" was made, Anne
Griffin visited us, and Hentz showed her how it worked.
She was impressed, and I heard her say: "Hentz, this is the
most remarkable thing I ever saw! Now tell me what it's
made of."

Hentz replied, "Old urinals, old enema bags, a leather
belt, part of an aluminum chair, adhesive tape, and fishing
line." Out of such lowly items my son had designed something
that would eliminate the necessity of asking others to do
everything for him.

Because Hentz had never been blessed with great patience,
I never ceased to wonder how he could watch Willie work
on these inventions without expressing bitterness. Occasion-

ally he would say, "If I had my hands, nothing on earth would stop me." It was just a statement, and not self-pity. When he thought up something that seemed especially exciting to make, he would say, "Gosh, I wish I had my hands!" But it was the same kind of wish he'd make when he used to say, "Gosh, I wish we had a cabin cruiser!"

He and Willie made holders for drinking glasses that enabled Hentz to tilt the glass as the liquids were drunk. They made a three-tube receiver and a code oscillator when Hentz became interested in ham radio. I learned the code so that I could take the messages when he was in bed, but we abandoned this project when Hentz started his law course. There are just so many hours in each day! When men who were ham radio operators heard about his interest, he was besieged with sincere offers of fine equipment. No matter what Hentz wants, there are many people eager to help him get it.

One day Hentz wanted to have Willie James take him to Macon to a show, or to some kind of entertainment. Hentz had fever and the weather was bad and I told him that I didn't think it wise to go. Hentz said, "If I let a little dab of fever keep me home the rest of my life, I might as well get in bed and not get out!"

"It isn't a little dab of fever," I replied, "and I don't think that missing *one* thing you want to do should upset you so much. The weather is bad, and you know that a severe cold will go very hard with you."

He was annoyed, and said, "I'm nearly a grown man, and I think I ought to be able to decide about such matters."

All of a sudden I was angry! The resentment he felt and the anger I felt were the same healthy, normal kinds we'd experienced before he was hurt. There was no mention of his accident, and I doubt if either one of us thought about it. We had a thorough family quarrel, and I think Hentz enjoyed it as much as I did. It was exactly what we needed. For a moment I couldn't believe that I'd let such a thing happen, but as I thought about it I said to myself, "Well, why not?" Hentz was the same person he had always been, and I was the same: only our *way* of life had been changed. My anger was an indication to me that in my thinking Hentz was a personality again, and not a boy faced with tragedy.

It was with some anger and great love that I said: "Hentz, there are many ways to become a tyrant, and the easiest way is to go through life with every whim gratified. You could be a dreadful tyrant—the intelligent ones are the worst, you know. I don't believe you want to become one, and if I can help it you won't become one. It would be easier for me to grant your every wish, but I must refuse you some things."

Our disagreements shock Fred—at least *my* part in them do. Fred has not denied Hentz's slightest wish since he was hurt. This may be all right for Fred, but not for Hentz and me.

When Hentz wasn't ill with a urinary infection, he went to as many places and events as he could. He attended church; he went shopping in Macon; he went to ball games; in fact, he did as much as many people who have all their physical strength.

I shall probably never know what goes on in Hentz's mind about many situations with which we were faced; but, judging from his complacency, he wasn't hurt by many of them as his mother was. I could go nowhere to escape the sudden little pangs. They always leaped at me when I was not prepared. The old chronic ones I had almost become accustomed to; I could take them to bed with me, and pray them away, or go to sleep and leave them. At other times, when I was with Hentz in a public place, or with guests at home, I couldn't let him see me wince.

One Sunday Fred, Hentz, and I were at church. Willie James always placed Hentz's chair immediately behind the back seat; between it and the little room that is opened when the church is crowded. Somebody always put a chair beside Hentz's chair for me. Because Fred usually ushers, and takes up the collection, he doesn't sit with us. The minister announced that we would stand and sing the hymn "Take My Life." I always felt a little self-conscious standing beside Hentz, and wondered if he thought about it. As the organ began the music I felt a sickening dread for the words I knew would follow.

I couldn't make a sound. I don't particularly care for the music of this song, I think it drags too much; and if the penitent one had so much enthusiasm for giving, it ought to be done in a livelier manner. With each note the singing congregation came nearer to the words I dreaded: "Take my life, and let it be Consecrated, Lord, to Thee; Take my moments and my days, Let them flow in ceaseless praise." The words that come next made me bow my head and ask God not to let Hentz mind too much: "Take my hands, and let them move At the impulse of Thy love; Take my feet, and let them be, Swift and beautiful for Thee."

In a voice that never faltered or weakened, Hentz sang to God about his hands and asked that his feet be swift and beautiful. How could Hentz sing that song? How *could* he?

In November, 1952, Hentz became very ill. There had been little relief from the urinary upsets, and they became more severe and lasted longer. There would be only two or three days' relief before another one came. The anxiety was great, and Fred and I were about physically exhausted. We would have to be up nearly all night fighting with the chills and subsequent fever. The fever always went above 105°. The urologist tried every new antibiotic that came out in an effort to stop the infections, but nothing seemed to help. Our life consisted of trying to get Hentz warm enough to stand the chill, and later cool enough to tolerate the high temperatures. We stood for hours bathing him in ice water or iced alcohol. It went on endlessly, day and night. My worry about his condition and my worry because he was disappointed over having his school work interrupted were constant company. One day he said, "Being in a wheel chair wouldn't be so bad if I didn't have to worry about pressure sores and these kidney attacks."

Our friends told us that they thought we were brave, but I felt unworthy of the praise. What was bravery? Fred said that if we were 100 per cent Christians we would not have suffered. I didn't agree with him because I don't believe one of the purposes of Christianity is to make you immune to suffering. It seemed that by now I should have been beyond feeling anything; but every new pain Hentz had, each new chill, was no easier for me than the previous one.

Hentz's condition became critical, and we took him to Macon to the hospital. He had been hospitalized many times since returning from New York, but this time I knew his condition was worse than it had ever been. The urologist had drugs flown to Macon that had not been put on the market, and with each new one our hopes mounted, but disappointment followed. Hentz was unconscious for the only time with the exception of the short period following his rescue from the lake. Each day seemed like the one before, and again the doctors despaired for Hentz's life.

I can't explain it now, but through all the long days and nights I knew Hentz would live. Anxiety is the most thorough punishment ever devised, but through all the awfulness of it I knew Hentz would live.

Hentz said many baffling things while he was so ill. Some would have been funny if he hadn't been in such a serious condition. One day he called me to his bed, and he sounded as though he were perfectly conscious. With eyes too far back in his head, and tortured with fever, he asked, "Mother, did you know that more crimes are committed by people who live on inclines than by any other group?"

That night two young friends of his, a boy and a girl, knocked softly on the door. I whispered to them that they could come in if they were very quiet. The three of us sat by the high white bed without speaking. Suddenly Hentz cried out, and I leaped to my feet and stood by his bed. In a voice filled with urgency, and with the same urgency on his face, he cried: "I've got to get out of here! I must get out! Please, somebody, let me out. I have so much to do! I can't spend my life in a hospital bed! I wish I could get away from this hospital and run and run and run. I wish I could run twenty miles without stopping!"

None of us spoke, and in a moment Hentz was very quiet and again in an unnatural sleep. It was the first time I'd heard him voice such feeling. Was this what he hid behind that bright smile? He didn't know what he'd said; but the words came from the deepest recesses of his being. It was indecent for us to hear them when he had no defenses.

I left the room and went to the adjoining bathroom. I looked in the mirror at myself as I prayed. I looked at my reflection so that I wouldn't cry. I asked God to give Hentz peace of mind, and to give me courage and strength to carry on until a better time came. I stayed in the bathroom until I felt calm, and then went back into the room. I tried to look cheerful, but when I looked at the young people I saw that they were both crying.

We knew we'd heard a wish wrung from Hentz's heart.

The next day, when I was alone in the room with Hentz, the door opened quietly and a young Presbyterian minister walked in. He was a man that I had heard much about; although he was very young he was one of the leading ministers in Macon. He had not been in Macon very long, and I had never met him before. He shook my hand and stood looking at Hentz a long time before speaking again. Hentz's pulse was so wild that the collar on his pajama coat was fluttering crazily.

After a long silence the minister said, "I know you must ask yourself a thousand times a day, 'Why?' Don't you?"

"No. I don't torment myself with questions. The thing I feel so terribly is the waste—the cruel waste."

"You are mistaken. There is no waste. If he were to die at this moment it would be a life gloriously spent. You don't know me, but I know all about Hentz. You have no idea of the number of people who talk to me and tell me what this boy has meant in their lives. Do you realize that the manner in which he has borne up under this tragedy has made his life have more meaning than it would have had otherwise? No, there has been no waste."

Such visits made us a little braver, and a little surer of the ultimate good that would come if we held fast.

Hentz's fever lessened, but he was still terribly thin and weak and sick. Because the urologist said that we would have to take him back to New York for surgery, we brought Hentz home from the hospital to try to strengthen him before the New York trip. We tried not to worry, because God had helped us through so many close places; and we knew He would help us through another.

The Perry people did everything in their power to tempt Hentz's poor appetite. They brought quail, squab, chicken, Florida fish, fine cakes, even venison. We knew that if he wouldn't eat the food we offered him here, it would be worse in the hospital in New York. Hentz was certainly not enthusiastic over going back to New York; but, like us, he knew that he must, and he tried to make the best of it.

Anne Griffin visited us before we left for New York. She always marveled at our crazy household, at the fun and the laughter, the company coming in at the back door and out at the front, with the telephone ringing amid the confusion. After this visit she tried, in a letter, to tell me how Hentz manages to make his handicap unimportant to other people. She wrote: "I loved your letter except for the news that Hentz is still having the urinary upsets. Oh, Harriet, I wish I could be God for only five minutes. I know He knows and does what is right, but I want Him to hurry. Hentz is so wonderful. When I'm with him I don't even think of his handicap, his mind is so alive and eager and stimulating."

Hentz, too, thinks we find real pleasure in living, because one day he said, "You know, I think we have more fun than other people, don't you?"

I didn't know quite what he meant, so I asked, "Fun? What kind of fun?"

He explained. "I think we laugh and enjoy things more

than a lot of other people. I think we have fun all the time."

Before we left for New York, I kept after him continually to *eat*. I wanted him to be stronger before he underwent surgery. Nothing I suggested in the way of food appealed to him. In near desperation I said: "Well, can you eat a candy bar? They are full of energy-giving ingredients, and it might pick you up considerably. Athletes eat a candy bar or two before the two-mile race, you know."

He looked at me with the nicest twinkle in his eyes, and in mock seriousness said, "Look, Hattie, we might as well face it. I'm no athlete."

It was this wonderful good humor of his that helped me get through the next bad place, and the next—and all the bad places that might yet be.

Before we went to New York, a man from another state came to see Hentz. He had heard about him, and was interested because he had also had a serious accident, although of much less severity than Hentz's. They had a good visit together, and as the man stood to leave he said: "My boy, keep your chin up! You can have a beautiful life."

Hentz looked the man straight in the eyes, held his head proudly, smiled, and answered:

"I am *having* a beautiful life."

During the last part of November, 1952, we were still in Perry. The doctors in New York and Macon decided it would be better for Hentz to stay in Perry until after the Thanksgiving holidays. Hentz was gaining strength, and began again to go places. On one of the trips to the Macon urologist the doctor said to me: "Mrs. Houser, Hentz was recently a desperately sick boy. How can he look as he does now?" I told him that it was Hentz's determination, and he agreed that it must be.

Charles came home for Thanksgiving, and he and Hentz went somewhere almost every night. Charles was disgusted because Hentz didn't remember that Charles had come from school to see Hentz when he was so ill. He thought it was a dreadful waste to make such a sacrifice and not have Hentz know it. Charles was having trouble with his back, and a doctor in Nashville thought he might have a ruptured disc. One night when they came home Hentz said he had new names for them: "Wreck Neck Houser and Crack Back Bledsoe." Hentz told Charles that he was going to ask Dr. Hill to do a laminectomy on Charles, then put him in a brace, and perform a couple of kidney operations. Hentz said he hoped that while all this was going on a pressure sore would develop—one of such proportions that it would have to be cleansed with a Plumber's Friend. Their humor got pretty rough at times, but it was grand to have Charles home.

Mildred and Dr. Hendrick decided it would be awful for Hentz to go to New York without a festive Thanksgiving dinner. I've forgotten why we didn't have one, but I think we thought we'd leave Perry on that day, and then our plans were changed. So Mildred cooked a tremendous turkey, made dressing, gravy, lemon pie, brought peach pickles, crab-apples, guava jelly, rolls, and many other things. I prepared the molded cranberry salad, rice, sweet-potato soufflé, ambrosia, and coffee. We had a wonderful coconut cake the minister's wife brought to Hentz, fruit cakes, charlotte, and many other desserts people had sent.

Mildred had the florist make a centerpiece for the table. It was a brown Pilgrim's hat with a wide gold ribbon and buckle on it, and it was filled with chrysanthemums, autumn leaves, pine cones, green squash, wheat, and tiny cattails. It was very striking. I got out our best linen, china, and silver. Mildred and Dr. Hendrick insisted that they were going to serve us, because I didn't have help that day, but I made them sit down and eat with us. We had invited Fred's mother and Louise and Leonora. It was truly a Thanksgiving dinner, and I know all of us had much to feel humble about; but that night my gratitude was for friends like them.

CHAPTER THIRTEEN

On our second flight to New York, on December 1, 1952, the wild hope and the excitement were missing. Hentz was going for surgery to a hospital where earlier he had spent many critical hours. There would be no enjoyable stay at the Institute; there would be nothing but sickness, transfusions, nausea, and discomfort. The surgeon who would do the operation was so skillful that our confidence was complete, but we dreaded it because we didn't know positively what was causing the trouble.

The ambulance drivers were men that Hentz had known on his previous trip, and their glad welcome improved his spirits. They took us to the hospital on Twentieth Street, and at the desk we found out that Hentz would not be put in the Miners' Ward. The surgeon had made arrangements for him to be on the same floor with his urological patients.

The days spent in that ward stand out as one of the more unhappy experiences we've had. The majority of the patients were old men. Hentz couldn't play his radio because it annoyed one man; he didn't have any of his gadgets that enable him to read in bed; and there was no TV in the ward. There was just the business of sickness and inactivity. This was no place for a boy of nineteen—with old men; he couldn't read or listen to music; he didn't know a soul, and he had no human being close by who cared a whit about him.

I was allowed to visit Hentz one hour in the morning, one hour in the evening, and only one hour on Sunday. His wretchedness, combined with his distressing physical condition and the austerity of his surroundings, caused me to develop a strong dislike for the hospital. Hentz acted cowed, and he didn't want to be a nuisance to these strangers who went about life with such businesslike precision. I tried to make him understand that the people were doing their job, and that their job was to take care of him and the other patients. But in a few days his fighting spirit had weakened to one of fear and nervousness.

Lottie, the therapist from Austria, who stayed with us in Perry, visited Hentz, and when she saw how the situation in the ward affected him she promised to try to get Hentz moved into the Miners' Ward. There at least he could play his radio, and watch TV in a more congenial atmosphere.

In a day or two Hentz was moved to the Miners' Ward, but he never felt at ease. He had a notion that he was put in the other ward because the nurses didn't want him in the Miners' Ward, and all the assurances that the urologist gave did not convince him.

I've read that man is more afraid of pain than of death, and I believe it. Hentz never seemed afraid of dying, but he was afraid of the pain he'd had in this hospital during the earlier part of the year. One night when I visited him he was suffering and fearful that the pain would grow more intense. I tried to talk to him to ease his mind, and he did look more relaxed.

In the bed next to Hentz was Nestor, a young boy who'd

been flown to New York from Puerto Rico for treatment. He was very charming and intelligent, and was helping Hentz with his Spanish. To get Hentz's mind off his pains and troubles, I began talking to Nestor. He had a nice smile, and appealed to me very much. I never did learn the cause of his paralysis, and perhaps he didn't know, either. He was paralyzed from his waist down. I asked him about their Christmas customs, and he had a wistful look on his face as he told me about them.

They don't have Santa Claus in Puerto Rico; they have the Three Kings, who bring gifts for the children. This happens on January 6th. From December 24th until January 6th is the holiday season, and the climax is the night the Three Kings come. During this time the family enters into activities as a group, and apparently they don't celebrate as we in the States do. The children have to cut grass and put it under their beds in a box. It is for the Kings' camels. Of course, the parents take it out and put their gifts there instead, saying the Three Kings left the gifts. I told him that he would certainly have some grass under his bed. He laughed and asked, "Where will you find grass during the winter in this vast acreage of asphalt?"

Nestor looked misty-eyed as he talked about his home. When I got back to the hotel I called Fred and said he must bring a shoebox full of grass when he came to New York. Fred usually manages to keep calm when I make my strange requests, but the box of grass perplexed him. When I told him it was for Nestor, who was so far from home for the first Christmas season in his life, Fred promised to find the very finest grass in Georgia. Nestor admitted that he still put grass under his bed, although he was twenty-one, and I confessed that we still hung our stockings. I think Fred has outgrown the desire, but Hentz and I won't let him quit. Odd, how a silly thing like making a confession can make you feel so much closer to someone. It's like finding someone who likes the same book or radishes or rain or watermelons.

For this stay in New York I had gone to the hotel where I first stayed on my previous visit. Because the doctors at the hospital said Hentz ought to eat more than he was eating I decided to go looking for another place where I could prepare food for him. I wanted to be near the hospital and at the same time get in a respectable neighborhood.

One day I decided to look for new quarters, and stopped in a nice-looking grocery store on the corner of Third Avenue and Twentieth Street. The store appeared to be privately owned, and I thought the proprietor might be able to help me. He was very kind, and a lovely-looking woman who was paying for her groceries overheard our conversation and began to talk to me. She began giving me directions, and then said, "But it will be simpler if you come with me." She took me to several places around Gramercy Park, and she knew people at all of them. I met many of her friends, and all were interested in helping me. After a while we found a room in a hotel that faced the park. The hotel was not very modern, but they assured me that nice people lived there. Though my room was pretty shabby, it had two large windows, and in one corner were a little stove and refrigerator. In addition, it cost less than the other hotel.

The friendly lady in the grocery store was Mrs. Earl Breeding, Executive Secretary for the Manhattan Council of Churchwomen. She lived a few doors from me at the National Arts Club. I learned something new every day— nothing very important, but interesting. She had taken me to a place that was owned by the Episcopal Church and where rooms could be rented. It was called Calvary House, and as we went in I asked, "Do I have to be an Episcopalian in order to stay here?" She laughed and replied: "Mercy, no! They aren't allowed to ask you. In New York it is forbidden to ask anyone his or her nationality or religion." It seemed to me that that was a stringent restriction to put on the Episcopalians. Suppose they *wanted* to use it for their church members? We met a pleasant lady there who regretted that there were no vacancies. She asked for Hentz's name, and instructions as to how to find him so that she could take him the altar flowers from the church. In a few days she invited Lois and me to have lunch with her.

Lois told me that the park in front of the hotel was the only one in New York with locks on the gates, and I thought that that was not in keeping with not being allowed to ask if I were an Episcopalian. Unless you own a key you can't get inside. Mrs. Breeding said that she would unlock the gates for me at any time I cared to go in. There wasn't anything in there to create a wild desire to crash the gates—I just didn't like to be locked out.

I loved this part of New York, and the houses reminded me of Charleston and Savannah. I always admired the heavy black lacquered front doors with the heavy brass knockers and doorknobs. I determined to lacquer our front door when I got back to Perry.

One of the bellboys—or bellmen, whichever they are—was from Augusta, Georgia. He helped me with my bags when Lois and I arrived from the other hotel, and he was very kind. I told him that I did not have dishes or cooking utensils in any of the suitcases, and he laughed and said he would see what he could find. He produced a weird assortment of china

and pewter knives and forks, but I was very proud of them.
That night I asked him where I could find a grocery store
that was open, and he gave me instructions. He said, "I'd
better go with you because you'll need help with your packages." I assured him that I could manage. However, I bought
more than I intended to, and when I started to leave the
store I realized that I *did* need help. Then I heard someone
say: "Give those to me. I can take them." It was the colored
man from Augusta. He had followed me to the store in order
to help me. When we reached the hotel, I offered him some
money for his kindness, but he didn't want to take it. He said:
"Thank you, but please don't feel that you have to give me
something every time I do anything for you. I want to do it.
We all have to live in this world together." So the next time
he did something nice for me, I gave him a book about Dr.
George Washington Carver.

Hentz's condition was a constant source of anxiety, and
his nervousness made life more difficult for us. I knew it was
the result of too much hospital. I tried to tell him that he was
just another case to the people who worked at the hospital,
and that when the help were whispering it was probably
about their own troubles, or a date they had had the night
before, or a show, but certainly not Hentz. His uneasiness
worried me, and annoyed me too. Most of the employees
were extremely kind. Whenever I visited he would be glad to
see me, but at the same time fearful that somebody might not
like it. I tried to remember how much he had been through,
and to realize that if he became cranky about some things
it was no more than we had reason to expect.

One Sunday afternoon when Tracy Horton and I were
sitting by the elevator waiting for the 2:00 P.M. visiting hours,
we saw a woman coming toward us with an armload of mag-

nificent white chrysanthemums. It was the lady from Calvary House with the flowers from the church. People like her compensated us for many other things.

After our visit Tracy and I left the hospital to get a bus to a Park Avenue Church where we were going to hear the *Messiah*, and we passed the National Arts Club. It looked so quaint and inviting that we went inside to look around. They were having the annual Book Fair, so we looked in on that, too. Tracy found Charles Allen's book *In Quest of God's Power*, and bought it for Hentz. I saw Mrs. Breeding and her husband, who invited me to dinner on Wednesday night to hear William L. Shirer and two other writers. I told them I could not go to dinner because I would be at the hospital, but I agreed to go later for the lectures.

Tracy and I got to church an hour early, so we sat in the chapel and read the book she had bought. I felt so peacefully quiet and relaxed in the beautiful building reading the book about God's eagerness to help us. I don't think Tracy or I spoke a word, but I was conscious of deep understanding. Friends like Tracy and Lois made God seem even closer, because there was never a need to hide or pretend with them. With some people you talked about the headlines in the paper, politics, or the economic upswing in the South, without mentioning faith and hope—not because you were ashamed of it, but because you couldn't bear to have it scorned or smiled upon indulgently.

As Tracy and I left the church at six-thirty, and walked down the cold, windy avenue, Tracy turned and said: "I want you to meet Axel. Let's go to see him!" I had heard her talk about this friend of hers, but his place in her life was a mystery to me. She said she had met him one day at Horn and Hardart's when they shared a table. I thought it sounded unconventional for a young lady so well brought up as Tracy; but they had continued the friendship. She said Axel had been a bouncer in a night club, a missionary, a teacher, a groomsman for the king's horses in Denmark, and was now a doorman at a supper club. On this cold night Tracy decided that she would simply have to see Axel in his blue doorman's uniform.

We rode crosstown buses and walked in the cold to find him. When we did, he certainly gave me a start! I don't know what I had expected, but it certainly was not what I found. I had wondered if there was some kind of strange romance in the friendship! Later Tracy told me that Axel was seventy, but he looked older. He was precious—Tracy had just said he was, "Cu-u-ute!" as she does when somebody is particularly wonderful. Axel had lost his upper teeth since she had seen him; though it made him look unusual it didn't detract one bit from his dignity. I've seen other people who have suffered the same loss that were obviously ill at ease; but Axel made no attempt to hide the vacancy with the palm of his hand or to laugh without opening his mouth. Nothing in his behavior made you think he even missed the departed companions to his lower teeth. His sleeves were much too long, because he was very slight and small of stature, and his doorman's hat looked as though it would cause him to topple over at any moment because it was so large and heavy; but everybody who entered or left the place showed Axel marked respect. With all the trappings for comedy, he managed to look regal.

Tracy asked him how he remained so cheerful, and he said, "Hope, faith, vision, and application." He said things that did me more good than anything I'd heard in ages. He said, "Of course your son can get well if he has faith in his heart."

He spoke with a very noticeable accent, and I had difficulty understanding him. He was deeply religious and very profound. It was shocking to be talking to a man about such things in the doorway of a smart eating place with noisy people going in and out. He said he wanted to go to the hospital to meet Hentz. He told us of the many times when he had been saved, according to him, by a miracle. He said doctors refused to believe some of the happenings, but he smiled and said, "That's because those doctors were lacking in imagination."

He beamed a toothless smile when I told him what a rewarding experience it was for me to meet him, and he followed us up the street a little way, but with one eye back on his doorway. The last thing he said was how happy he was that I thought he had helped me, because that was the thing that gave meaning to his life—hoping to help others.

Tracy gathers to herself the strangest mixture of people, and I went with her to many out-of-the-way places to see some of her friends. Some were people working in little restaurants who'd told her about a sick child; some were talented people who had not been able to make things work out right in New York. A day or two after our visit with Axel, I met her at Columbia and found her engaged in the most unusual activity of all. She was out in the middle of Broadway helping an old trash man pick up the trash. His cart had overturned once, and he had gathered everything together, only to have it tilt again. Tracy walked out among the cars and assisted the poor soul to pick up the debris again. She looked as though it wasn't unusual at all for a young lady to gather up trash in the middle of Broadway. When I said something to her about it, she said, simply, "It turned over twice."

Hentz's birthday was approaching, and he said he didn't

want me to bring a birthday cake or any presents to the hospital. He said one of the other patients had had a birthday a few days earlier and someone just said, "Happy birthday," and that was the end of it. I love birthdays and Christmas, and such enforced austerity would be a sacrifice for me. These notions that Hentz had were all a part of his feeling about the hospital, and I prayed that if we ever got home again we could stay there. Something happened to Hentz's personality the minute the wheels of the plane touched down in New York. I think it was because the State of Georgia was paying the expense of the New York hospitalization, and in Macon and Atlanta and other places Fred paid it. I tried to explain that nobody cared, or probably didn't even know anything about this part of our problems. Then I would look at Hentz and think of the pride we valued so highly and of how uncomfortable it could make us at times. I couldn't decide whether I wanted him to accept help as though he deserved it, or to accept it with difficulty. There were disadvantages in both attitudes. We had not asked for help from the State, but the people in charge kept in close touch with us and knew when Hentz was not doing well. When they heard of Hentz's critical condition in Macon, they telephoned to us that if we needed to take Hentz to New York immediately to go ahead, and that they would finance the trip. They said we need not wait for the usual forms and papers to be filled out. That kind of support removes the terror from difficult situations. We never had to wonder if Hentz would die because we couldn't pay for expensive New York surgeons and hospital care.

One night after I had visited Hentz, and was on the elevator going to my room, the elevator man showed me a picture of his wife. Though she certainly was no beauty, I said something appropriate about her face showing strength of character. He said, "She is the most wonderfulest woman I ever knew." I told him it was grand for him to think so. She was born in France, he said, completely blind. Her sight came to her suddenly when she was grown. He said that it was a miracle, and that even the doctors admitted that it was a miracle. He put the picture back in his billfold and, with tenderness in his eyes, said: "She crochets—my, how she can crochet! Some women think they've done something when they crochet a little derlie, but my wife makes bedspreads, mats, chair-backs—she even crocheted all the curtains in the house." A quick mental picture flashed through my mind of what the house must look like with all that crocheting! As I was getting off the elevator, he said, "I like to hear Southern women talk, and all of them I've known was so friendly."

He was a huge man, and he said he had superhuman "strenth." One night Tracy and a friend of hers named Matthew were returning home with me to have some coffee and to talk. The elevator man wanted to show Matthew some of his "strenth." Matthew is very dignified, in a delightful sort of way, and he was getting his Ph.D. in English at Columbia. The huge man was showing Matthew some kind of trick—judo or something—and before we knew it it looked as though Matthew would be upside down in the elevator. The big man's heart was as big as he was, however, and every time he saw me he asked about Hentz. He always said, "Your son will be all right," because he believed in miracles. He bought a very lovely card and sent it to Hentz, and the writing on the card was exquisite. It was so delicate, that it seemed odd that such a huge man had written it.

It *was* heartwarming to have people show an interest in our problems.

On December 12th, Hentz's birthday, I did as he instructed and didn't bring him a birthday cake. But after lunch one of the nurses came marching into the ward holding high a very lovely birthday cake, with the candles blazing. Some of the nurses had had it made for him, and I thought it was so kind of them. The nurses must have been disappointed. Though he was happy to discover that they had done such a nice thing for him, he was a little embarrassed for the other boy, who hadn't been treated in the same manner. Hentz spent his nineteenth birthday in a hospital, as he had done on his eighteenth. They were nothing alike, however. In the previous instance there were friends and a surprise party, and the hope that before long he would be well. This time there was the prospect of surgery, and little likelihood that Hentz would be well in the immediate future.

Hentz's eleventh operation was to take place on December 15th. Fred said it was almost impossible for him to come, so we sent for Parks again. Lois and Tracy were there too. Hentz was in worse physical condition at this time than he had been before any surgery. The long sickness at home had weakened him. It was a dangerous operation for a strong person, and more especially so for Hentz.

Tracy, Lois, Parks, and I were not allowed in the ward as they prepared Hentz for surgery. We were on the bench by the elevator when I saw the stretcher being rapidly rolled toward us by a man in a green operating-room gown. I hurried toward the stretcher so that I could say a word or two to Hentz before he was whisked away. I wished I could say the things to him that were in my heart. Hentz looked up at me, smiling, and said in a very low voice so that the orderly wouldn't hear him: "I'm afraid, and I don't know why. I've never been afraid before." Although he laughed, I knew he meant it.

I touched his head and said: "Please don't be afraid. The same God who has taken you through all the others will take care of you now. Of that I'm convinced." I think that Hentz was afraid of the pain and discomfort that he knew would follow, but at the time I thought he meant something else.

The greedy elevator door closed, separating me from him again. They were always taking him to some indefinite place where I couldn't help him, and where I wondered if he were frightened. But his smile, as the elevator door closed, was as big as any of the others had been.

We had been waiting about forty-five minutes when the elevator stopped and Hentz was rolled out. The orderly was going so fast that I didn't have a chance to ask any questions. I knew he could not have had the operation, because kidney operations take several hours.

In a few seconds the surgeon appeared. He was dressed in a dark blue cashmere suit with a pearl-gray vest. There was a gardenia in his lapel. He assured me that Hentz was all right. He said: "I don't like Hentz's looks today. The operation will be at 2:00 P.M. tomorrow."

I asked if he thought there would be a change by tomorrow.

He answered, "Oh, yes. Hentz was very nervous." As he entered the elevator, he turned back and said something to me that removed almost all the fear I had about the operation. He said: "I told Hentz that there would be three of us in that operating room tomorrow. There will be Hentz, me, and God. Don't worry. Everything will be all right." He smiled reassuringly as the door closed. Just knowing that the surgeon knew that his skill could be supplemented by God's help made me relax.

When we could see Hentz he said the operation was postponed because the X-ray pictures had been lost. Someone had suggested to the surgeon that new ones be made, and that he go on with the operation, but he had refused to do so without the pictures he had studied. It proved to be a happy mistake because the next day Hentz was almost eager to get the operation over with.

The hours were long and the strain was great, but beneath it I felt the assurance of God's presence. After many hours had passed, the surgeon stepped out of the elevator and stood before the four of us. He looked worried, and there were lines around his mouth. He had on his operating-room attire. He hastened to assure me that Hentz was all right; but then he said: "I found the kidney tubercular. I did not remove it. Probably a more daring man would have done so, but I didn't see it that way."

CHAPTER FOURTEEN

The second Christmas season since Hentz's accident was a far cry from any I'd ever known. I missed the hectic days of selecting the proper tree, making fruit cakes, and decorating the house. I missed Fred and I missed my home. As never before, I sympathized with lonely people in ugly hotel rooms in big cities during Christmas. There ought to be a living room with a fireplace and a tree reaching to the ceiling. There ought to be scurrying to the attic to bring down precious ornaments that had been collected through the years since your son was a little fellow. There ought to be thousands of bright-colored glass balls and pine cones and painted magnolia leaves and pine leaves and holly. There ought to be mistletoe over the front door. There ought to be concern over the decoration on the front door that is to be judged by the committee from the garden club who on Christmas Eve would choose the one to get the coveted prize. There ought to be secrets about gifts, and there ought to be the visiting of relatives, neighbors, and friends. And there certainly ought to be confusion.

There was none of that for me during Christmas, 1952.

There *was* a fireplace in my room, but it had long been sealed. However, the mantel could be used effectively. I crowded the bright Christmas cards I received on the mantel, and was pleased with the effect. When the shelf was covered I began stringing the cards on cord and made swags all around the room. It cheered me to see the colorful reminders that many friends were thinking of me during this trying time. I didn't want to buy Christmas decorations for the shabby room for me alone to see.

One day the maid was in my room, standing motionless in the middle of the floor, with her broom propped under her chin. She turned slowly and looked at every wall. When she faced me I saw that there were tears in her eyes.

"Just look at these thousands and thousands of cards!" she exclaimed. Of course, there were not that many. "My, how fortunate you are! Guess how many I received."

I said I had no idea.

"Four. I didn't get but four." She put her face in her hands and cried.

I was embarrassed and ashamed. I wanted to say something to help her. "But you're from Jamaica, and you live in a huge city. I'm from a small town where we know every man, woman, child, and dog. You see, that makes a tremendous difference. You haven't been in New York very long, have you?"

Wearily she answered, "I've been here thirty-two years."

All I could do was mumble, "I'm sorry."

As soon as she left the room, I put on my hat and coat and went out to buy my first and only Christmas card! I bought the prettiest one I could find. Then I went to the little Perfumer's Shop in Gramercy Park and bought her two very frivolous gifts. I hope so much that she was made a little happier.

New York was awesome in its lovely holiday regalia. Everyone ought to see Fifth Avenue during the Christmas days. One night after dinner with Mrs. Breeding and friends of hers we took a Fifth Avenue bus and rode up to Central Park. I marveled at the talent and time that was used in making every shop and store as beautiful as it could be. The lions in front of the Library looked silly and uncomfortable with wreaths intertwined with red lights around their necks. They seemed disgusted with such undignified doings. After that night I rode up the shining avenue every opportunity I had. I heard people on the buses saying, "They've commercialized Christmas until it has lost its meaning." If the dazzling sight that I could see from the bus window was commercialization, then I liked it!

There were times when I was worried and frightened, but I was never really lonely in New York. A bus ride cured loneliness for me because I liked to watch the people. At home there were two classifications: variations of the Anglo-Saxon and variations of the Negro. In New York people have strange faces, wear strange clothes, and talk strange languages. I didn't even mind the weather, and the previous stay and this one were the first times I had been out of the South during the winter.

A few days before Christmas, as I was walking crosstown on Twentieth Street toward the hospital, I saw an old woman approaching me. As she neared, she slowed her uncertain steps and looked into my eyes. I must have smiled a little because she stopped. Her head was wrapped in a shabby shawl. Her back was stooped and her face was wrinkled. She looked lost, and I thought she was going to ask directions from me. And I hoped that I would be able to assist her. By now I was feeling pretty cocky about getting around in New York City.

In very broken English she said, "Please tell me where the hospital is."

We were near Third Avenue, so I pointed to the Columbus Hospital.

She said that she had been there, and that it was not the one she wanted. Then I told her that I was going to the New York University Hospital, and that she could go along with me.

Tears came into her eyes, and she got out a dingy handkerchief to wipe them away.

"I'll help you if I can. What's the matter?"

Then she told me something that made me forget about Hentz and our problems. Her husband had been in a hospital for a week, and she could not find him. She had been walking throughout New York, from hospital to hospital, looking for him. Evidently she had not learned the name of the hospital when he was taken away. She must have thought there was only one in the city. I took her by the arm and told her to go with me. She walked with difficulty, and she said her feet hurt very badly. I looked down at them, and they were gnarled and arthritic and knotty, in run-over shoes.

As we crept along she told me of her long search. I tried to imagine how I'd feel if Fred and I were in a strange land and he was in a hospital in some big city. Suppose I too were looking for Fred, and didn't know the language and couldn't make anyone understand?

I took her to the information desk of the University Hospital; but the girl there told me that the old lady had already been there, and that her husband was not in the hospital. I told the girl about finding the wretched little woman on the streets and how upset she was, and I asked if there was any place where she could get help. The girl shrugged and said that every day people came there looking for members of their families. Then and there I determined to stay with my new friend until we'd found her husband.

After a while another woman stepped up to the desk and heard our problem, and she began to speak to the little old lady in a foreign language. In that way we learned the name of the husband's doctor. It was a name that was very common in New York, and that would involve many telephone calls. From the desk we went to an office in the hospital where a volunteer Red Cross worker started to work on the problem. She made many telephone calls, and I could tell she was getting the desired information. She was very kind to the little woman, and that made me happy. I didn't leave until she assured me that she had the name of a member of the family, and was in touch with the lost husband's doctor.

By this time visiting hours at the hospital were almost over, and I saw by the clock that I had five minutes to spend with Hentz. I told the little old woman that I hoped she would have a wonderful Christmas, and that her husband would be in good health. She took my hands in her roughened, chapped hands, and looked up at me with tears of relief and gratitude pouring down her cheeks. She said something that I did not understand. I did understand the look she gave me, and I knew then that that woman's upturned face compensated for all that I had thought I was missing of Christmas. It didn't take me as long to help her as it would have to make a measure of cookies or candy to send to a neighbor—and the joys aren't comparable. At last I began to have the Christmas spirit! I would never have had it had I continued thinking of nothing but my own troubles.

I dashed into the usually depressing ward, and was gratified to see that the tube from the Wangensteen pump was no longer in Hentz's nose, and that the glucose and blood had been discontinued. I told him that he had looked like a switchboard with all those tubes connected to him. There was just time to say hello and goodbye; then, as an afterthought, I asked him if I could bring him anything when I came back that night.

He grinned, and said: "Yes. Bring me a big bowl of ravioli."

On Christmas morning I was up at 4:00 A.M. to go to La Guardia to meet Fred. I had told him over the telephone that I'd meet him, but he had no idea that I meant it. How relief swept over me as I stood there in the cold dawn and saw Fred coming down the steps of the plane! Because he was loaded with packages, he couldn't wave at me, but he smiled. Odd, how I always feel a little timid when I meet Fred after not having seen him for such a long time. He told me that the packages were last-minute gifts the Perry people had sent to Hentz and to me. I wished I didn't have to tell Fred that Hentz's kidney was tubercular, but I knew I couldn't bear it alone any longer. We took a taxi back to New York so that we could talk. We discussed friends, Christmas presents, and the weather—and it was not until the taxi driver finished paying the man at the toll bridge and drove on across the bridge that I told Fred. I could see his face in the dim light, and the flexing of the muscles in his jaws. He was fighting for control to say the thing I knew he would say:

"Well, we'll come out of this some way. We've been faced with worse than this many times, and come through." Although I knew Fred said the thing I wanted to hear, the correct thing and the kind thing, always, it was heartening to hear the conviction in his voice.

As soon as visitors were allowed at the hospital, we were there. Hentz was pleased with all his gifts, and there were much talk and laughter. Hentz showed us a picture of Henry the Goat taken with Dr. Taft's little boys, and it made me feel how much time had passed to see how Henry had matured. There was a handsome check from Dr. and Mrs. Hendrick for a present to Hentz. One of the nurses saw it; and Hentz laughed and said, "Just think: in some places people have to pay their doctors!"

Lois and Albert had invited us to their home in Port Washington for Christmas dinner, but we told them we did not want to be so far from Hentz on Christmas day. A friend in Albert's office offered his apartment so that Lois and Albert could have us to dinner. The man said he would be away from New York during the holidays and it would make him happy to have a part in making our day nicer. The apartment was on the corner of Lexington and Twenty-second Street. Lois and Albert and Steve, their little boy, brought turkey, dressing, and all the wonderful things that go with Christmas dinner, from their home. I wanted to help, so Lois let me prepare avocado salad and French dressing, candied sweet potatoes and ambrosia—the ambrosia was a requisite for Southerners, she'd heard.

I prepared the foods in my little quarters, and Fred and I looked very small-townish and neighborly, walking around the park at sundown, loaded with pans and dishes. I thought we would be doing the same thing had we been at home. The very proper doorman at the apartment looked down his nose at us, but when we told him who was expecting us he was cordial and helpful.

Lois and Albert had also invited a dear old man who would have had to spend Christmas alone. He was a retired Congregational minister who'd had a long career preaching, and teaching at Harvard. He was good company, and we loved to hear his stories.

As we gathered around the dinner table Lois and Albert asked us to join hands, and they led us in singing an old hymn that went like this: "We bear the strains of earthly care, But we bear it not alone—" I noticed the mistiness in the others' eyes when we raised our heads.

After dinner Fred and I returned to the hospital. I had not said anything more to the surgeon about Hentz's condition; I was waiting for Fred to do it. As we sat by Hentz's bed talking, I saw the surgeon in the hall and motioned to Fred to go talk to him. I stayed with Hentz and tried to talk naturally, although my heart was in my throat.

After what seemed like ages, I saw Fred coming toward us, and he was smiling. I admired him for his performance. While Hentz was talking to someone else, Fred whispered that the surgeon had told him that the report had just come back from the laboratory, and that it showed that the kidney was not tubercular. The surgeon had removed two abscesses from the kidney which had been causing the trouble, but they showed no tuberculosis. I couldn't believe it; I thought he was only telling me that to make me happy. At last he produced the report from the laboratory. There were few words in it that made sense to me, but the ones I needed to understand were there. I bowed my head and my tears splashed on the yellow laboratory report in my lap.

When I raised my head Christmas was everywhere! My heart was singing lines from the Christmas carols I loved: "Hark! the herald angels sing," "All is calm, all is bright," "Yet in thy dark streets shineth the everlasting light. The hopes and fears of all the years Are met in thee tonight." This was the best day of all to have my prayers answered— the birthday of Jesus.

CHAPTER FIFTEEN

The surgeon dismissed Hentz from the hospital in New York on January 1st, 1953. Fred remained in New York to fly home with us. When we reached Perry we discovered that Felton, Charles, Louise, and Leonora had a brightly lighted Christmas tree in Hentz's room. Even though Christmas was gone, and the day had come to take down the decorations they thought a tree was appropriate. It was good of them to go to so much trouble—even though they overturned the TV while trimming the tree. Felton and Charles had gone to the freezer locker and had bought a kidney. They opened it and packed it with rocks. It was elaborately wrapped in holiday paper. Another gift was a big fish with firecrackers protruding from all sides. Something they'd read in 'Lil Abner about a loaded bloater had amused them, and Hentz. Hentz had high fever from a urinary infection, and didn't think the kidney was very funny; in fact, he gagged when he saw it. When he felt better he thought it was clever.

We were home again. Christmas was behind us; the operation was behind us; the future was before us. The future meant that Hentz would go back to school.

After the Christmas holidays ended Hentz returned to

Mercer, but his attendance was not regular because of the recurring urinary infections. They became more and more frequent, and he had to spend much time in the hospital in Macon. Because his fever would go to 106 and he could not take nourishment, it was necessary for him to be in the hospital to be given blood and glucose. Sometimes the illnesses would last a week, sometimes longer. As soon as he was dismissed from the hospital, he would enter into activities with a feverish intensity. He was embarrassed at having to return to the hospital with such frequency, and we would try to slip off and not let people know we'd gone. He was afraid people would think he was neurotic! Though I tried to explain that neurotics couldn't run temperatures as high as the ones he had, his sensitivity increased with each hospitalization. If we got home from Macon on Saturday night, he would go to church on Sunday to prove that he was not ill. I've seen him go with a fever of 103, and we couldn't force him to stay home without doing him more damage than the outing would do. He drove himself to great extremes —probably to convince himself that he was all right. When he was asked how he felt, he always replied, "Very fine, thank you—and how are you?" He did it so habitually that he would not even tell the doctors how wretched he felt at times. The urologist in Macon, who takes such a deep interest in Hentz, told me that he was so far from being neurotic that treating him was nearly as difficult as working with patients with imagined ailments.

After this trip to New York we had another urologist. Dr. McCall is one of the most dedicated doctors I've ever known, and Hentz and his problems presented a challenge to him. He read and studied everything he could find dealing with the problems of quadriplegics, and got in touch with men who had made studies of such problems. We liked the way he kept trying one thing after another—always feeling that somehow the problems could be worked out.

During the last of February, 1953, the urologist told us that Hentz couldn't go on having the urinary infections: he couldn't live unless something was done to relieve them. So Hentz had his twelfth operation. The urologist replaced the suprapubic tube—we should not have tried to get along without it. We thought Hentz would be out of school for two weeks; but complication after complication developed, mainly because Hentz insisted upon leaving the hospital before the doctor wanted to dismiss him. Hentz had to return to the hospital for a stay of two or three weeks.

One day Hentz said: "I might as well be realistic about it; I don't suppose I can go to college. Every time I try, I have to drop out and lose credit for my work. Perhaps it will be wiser to see about extension courses."

After the twelfth operation the infections were less severe, but they continued. Late in 1953 a new antibiotic was made available that put an end to the infections and accompanying discomforts. The drug and the improved method of bladder drainage gave Hentz the relief we had prayed for. Now, for the first time since the accident he was no longer plagued with chills and high fever.

After Hentz decided it would be impractical for him to continue to go to school, Fred told him that he needed him very much in his business. Because Fred's business had expanded, he had to have assistance, and he'd rather have Hentz than anyone else. Fred turned most of the insurance end of his business over to Hentz and Betty Hartley, a girl who is a year or two younger than Hentz, and who possesses an abundance of steadiness, intelligence, and capability. When Hentz first started going to the office, he wouldn't ask Betty to assist him with anything, but in her quiet, tactful way she helped, and now he lets her do things for him that he would accept from few people. Both are enthusiastic about the insurance business, and study and take courses in order to learn everything they can. Fred insists that Hentz take on the responsibilities of calling Atlanta about complicated coverages and tricky losses. Fred's office is next door, and he can help Betty and Hentz when they need him.

When Hentz's health improved so greatly, he ordered a motorized wheel chair so that he could go to town without having Willie James put him in the car or push his other wheel chair. I've never seen Hentz so excited over anything as he was about the prospect of the chair's arrival. Every time he heard a truck he would ask one of us to go to the door to see if the chair had come.

When the fine chair came, I've never seen Hentz more pleased. It meant freedom! Infirmities don't matter if they don't destroy freedom—and a spirit like Hentz's had to have it, and would find it in spite of all obstacles.

Hentz and Willie James at once went to work to make the chair operable for Hentz. Because his left arm was the stronger one, he had ordered a chair with a left-arm drive. It is guided by moving the arm. Hentz now put a little rod into the switch, and inserted the rod through a slot in a leather strap that is fastened to his hand. In this way he can push the lever forward and back. I've never seen a face happier than his when he came back from his first excursion alone. He said: "This is wonderful! Now I can go to town alone. Just think—alone!"

One day Hentz came home from town in his electric chair and said he had something special for me. He came into the dining room where I was and maneuvered his chair until he was facing me. The afternoon sun was coming through the window on the old pine hunt board, and on Hentz's hair. He told me to look in the little compartment behind the chair and take out the record and put it on the record player without looking at the title of the song.

When the music began I recognized it as a song that was always a particular favorite of ours, even before Hentz was hurt. It was the lovely song from *Carousel*, "You'll Never Walk Alone." As the chorus sang, "When you walk through the rain hold your head up high and don't be afraid of the storm," I knew Hentz was trying to tell me with this record that he didn't feel alone, and that the storms hadn't beaten him.

During 1953 Hentz began teaching a Sunday-school class. He had twenty-one boys and girls about nine and ten years old. It was a revelation to me that he was so fond of children. He came home beaming over the things they said to him, and he loved the teaching. His pupils think they are the favored group in the church to have him for a teacher. One little girl went home breathless one Sunday and said to her mother, "Guess what, Mother! I sat *close* to him today!"

Hentz told me one Sunday morning that he had to read a few words at church that evening. He had spoken on one other occasion in public since he was hurt, but I hadn't heard him because he spoke at a district youth meeting.

Fred and Hentz went to the church ahead of us. Anne was visiting, and she, Louise, Leonora, and I went later.

When we reached the church it was packed, and we were

escorted to seats near the front by Cub Scouts. I saw Hentz in his wheel chair near the organ, and Fred sitting close by on the front pew. Ten or twelve men who were on the scout committee, of which Hentz was chairman, were seated in chairs near the pulpit. The boy who would be made an Eagle Scout that evening was seated in front of us, holding his head erect above the colorful merit badges across his chest. I looked at his mother and father, and knew the pride that was theirs.

The lights were turned off, and a spotlight from the balcony was focused on the people around the pulpit. One of the men on the committee arose and stood behind the lectern and began to read. I don't remember what he read because I was watching Hentz.

I was afraid that I might cry and I looked out the stained-glass window that was behind Hentz—the one dedicated to his great-grandfather. Five years ago, in this very church, Hentz had been made an Eagle Scout. He was fifteen then. I remembered something silly: Hentz had been apprehensive because I had told him that when he pinned the tiny eagle on my lapel I was going to say, "Now I really *am* Mother Bird!"

I wished I could think of something else silly because I didn't feel so choked up then. While I was trying to think of something, a high-school boy, holding a candle, walked to the front of the church and handed the taper to someone to hold while he rolled Hentz's chair to the front. Because Hentz couldn't hold the candle, as he was supposed to do, the boy stood beside him holding it for him. The committee-man sat down.

Now, in a voice that was startlingly clear and strong, Hentz began to read. His composure and ease were unbelievable. He sounded just as he always sounded when he could stand before people to talk. I gripped the psalm book tightly as I heard Hentz read:

"'I represent the Spirit of Devotion to Others.

"'You have heard that if you would serve God well, you must serve well your fellow man. No one can live entirely unto himself. All are dependent upon others in greater or lesser degree. From the moment of your birth you were cared for by others. Even when you became old enough to do many things for yourself, you still depended upon others for education, guidance, and leadership. When you were given positions of leadership and responsibility at home, at school, or within the Troop, you had to depend upon the help of others to see each task successfully completed.

"'Now you have arrived at the mountain top of the Scouting Trail. It now becomes your privilege to look about you and see the beauty and grandeur of the land through which you have traveled. As you look you will see many others who are back along the Scouting Trail—some just starting the climb and others who are just behind you struggling to reach the top. Just as you have been helped, so must you go back along the Trail to help others to reach the top, for they depend upon you for help.

"'But another responsibility is yours. As you lead the way, so will others follow. It is your sublime privilege to set the example for your brothers—those who are Scouts and those who would be Scouts.

"'Remember that Scouting is the greatest brotherhood of youth the world has ever seen. Scouts are brothers to all and stand ready to serve others at all times. It has been truly said that if you would find your life, you must lose your life in the service to others.'"

I watched Hentz's still hands as he signaled to the high-school boy to light the candles for him, and I thought my heart would stop because of the sorrow and the beauty of what I saw.

Someone introduced the judge who would make the presentation of the Eagle badge. He stood near Hentz as he spoke. I looked at the two of them, and Hentz's disability seemed accentuated by the vigor and physical perfectness of the other man. The judge was dark and suntanned, and Hentz looked very fair by contrast. Suddenly I realized that the judge was gazing on Hentz as he talked. I remembered the many kindnesses shown us by this man, who was one of our closest friends, and the attentions he had shown to Hentz. He had seen, at very close range, Hentz's courage. I remembered words the judge had spoken several times in public: "The greatest force for good in my entire life has been Hentz Houser. No person, no sermon, no book, and no experience has ever had the spiritual impact for me that the quiet courage of this boy has had."

The judge was concluding his speech: "Taking part in this service tonight were Francis Nunn, Horace Evans, Allen Whipple, and Eagle Scout Hentz Houser. . . ." He mentioned others.

But Eagle Scout Hentz Houser was all I heard.

Life for us was wonderfully lacking in anxiety. Hentz's physical condition seemed splendid; he was anxious to go places and do things that other people did—and we wanted that for him too. But there was always the struggle, for Fred and me, to keep Hentz from developing a serious self-consciousness about the wheel chair and the attendant. Many times I've had to fight for self-control in the face of rudeness and curiosity. In New York Hentz didn't mind going to public places because there you see so many handicapped people. But in Macon and Atlanta and smaller towns they are rare. Sometimes I would follow behind Hentz and his attendant, and I resented the curious stares of the people passing on the street. The better bred ones waited until Hentz passed to turn and look, but others would stop dead-still to stare. I wanted to shield him from this kind of thing, but how could I?

At one time I did frighten a curious person. Hentz, his attendant, and I were in the Macon Hospital, where we had been visiting. Near the entrance we met a doctor, who was a friend of ours, and we were talking. A woman passing by saw Hentz, and stopped. Hentz happened to say something, and the woman turned to me and said, "Oh, he can talk!" I was furious, and afraid that she would say something to Hentz, so I said, "Yes, and he bites too!" She departed quickly.

Hentz once said: "I wish I didn't mind going places to buy things. I feel so obvious when people stare. A while ago a woman with two or three children passed me, and kept looking back. I heard her say to the children, 'My, we don't know what we have to be thankful for!'"

I asked, "What did she look like—intelligent or ignorant?"

How good to hear him laugh! "To be perfectly honest about it, *she* didn't look as though she had very much to be thankful about!"

Some of us, in order to keep our spiritual gifts in good condition, have to cling to some of the things that moth and rust can corrupt. I believe in such supports, and have lost fear and gained strength from some of mine that have a special meaning: a little brass bowl that Hentz gave me; a coral-colored hat that I bought in New York and wore to the hospital, and that Hentz said he liked; the redbud tree Hentz planted for me when he was a little boy—the electric blanket that Hentz had someone buy for me on my first birthday following his accident.

Recognizing this need has made me understand Hentz better. One day, after a trip to the attic, Fred came down and said: "Hentz, you ought to give some of that camping equipment to some little boy who needs it. There's so much stuff up there not being used that it seems wasteful. You ought to give your shoe skates to someone, and your golf clubs."

Hentz said a little stiffly, "If you don't mind, I'd like to keep them."

How well I understood! I used the perfume Hentz had given me on the Mother's Day before he was hurt sparingly; I couldn't bear to think of the bottle being empty. One day, when I was in his old room upstairs, I decided to give some of the books Hentz had when he was a child to some poor little boy. As I gathered them up, I suddenly knew I couldn't part with them. I had saved them through the years so that his children might read them—just as Hentz had read the set of tattered red volumes that had been Fred's when he was a little boy. If I admitted to myself that Hentz would never have children, I was surrendering! Why talk about faith and act as though you had none?

A few days later Hentz said: "Mother, I hate to have Pop think I'm selfish, but if I give all those things away it will be admitting that I'm licked. And I'm not!"

I said: "I know. I know."

In the late summer of 1953, two doctors from the Institute of Physical Medicine and Rehabilitation stopped in Perry to see Hentz. They had just visited Warm Springs and were enthusiastic about the work being done at the Foundation with paralyzed hands. They suggested that we get an appointment with Dr. Bennett, to see if anything more could be done for Hentz.

Dr. Bennett gave Hentz an appointment in Atlanta. Willie James wheeled Hentz into one of the examination rooms, put him on the table, and then came outside, where we waited for more than an hour and a half.

After the doctor came out, I went inside to see Hentz, and found him smiling happily. The doctor—one of the best in his field in the world, a man who had made a specialty of paralyzed hands, and a doctor of high repute among his colleagues throughout the country—was highly pleased with Hentz's little hand gadget. Hentz had brought it to Atlanta to show him, and now the doctor wanted him to go to Warm Springs and stay there for two months, have therapy, and to work to improve the device with more refined materials than the ones he had originally used.

Hentz began going to Warm Springs in late February or early March of 1954. He did not want to go as an in-patient, however, because he had had more than his share of hospitalization. He told the doctor and the therapist that we would drive to Warm Springs from Perry when they wanted to see him. The days of the visits were hectic indeed. If they wanted to see Hentz at nine, we would have to get up at 5:00 A.M. in order to get him dressed, and allow two hours for the drive. We had a new attendant for Hentz now. Willie James had moved to Florida—after his charming manner had persuaded every merchant in Perry and Macon to sell him merchandise on credit. Hentz would lie down on the reclining seat for the drive, and would be asleep almost immediately. The attendant—who could not drive—would be asleep a few minutes later, and Frieda, a lovable red dachshund that Dr. and Mrs. Hendrick had given to Hentz for a Christmas present, would curl up beside Hentz and follow suit.

The first trip we made to Warm Springs occurred the day after a tornado had passed through part of the state. Upon driving through the area, I saw people standing around a spot where a house had once stood. The ugly black storm had left only crumbled wreckage. When we came back late that afternoon, much of the pulverized foundation had been removed. A week later we drove to Warm Springs again. Where bricks and splintered wood had lain, we now saw a proud new house! How could such a thing so quickly have come to pass? Then I knew. Surely the neighbors of those stricken people were like our neighbors. They had come with nails and saws and hammers and planes and lumber and rebuilt the house for their friends. Every time I passed that new house I felt a surge of happiness at the knowledge that people are fundamentally good.

One Sunday morning Guy Hutcherson, our minister, and Bishop Arthur J. Moore, of the Methodist Church, came to see Hentz. We were particularly anxious to see Bishop Moore, because he had only recently returned from North Africa, and had seen Margery. Hentz tried to show the interest he felt, but I saw that he was quite pale. Bishop Moore told us that Margery was well, and full of plans for her forthcoming marriage to a man she'd met in Paris while going to school.

Hentz went to bed when the visitors left, and for six days he gagged and heaved. He could retain nothing in his stomach. He lost weight so rapidly that he looked worse than he ever had. We were dreadfully alarmed, and begged him to go to the hospital in Macon. After days of fighting a return to the hospital, Hentz finally consented.

When the doctor examined Hentz, he asked him and us many questions. There was no fever, nothing but violent nausea and dizziness. Finally the doctor said: "I believe his trouble is a disturbance of the inner ear. Ninety-nine per cent of the cases of this kind of nausea are caused by that. In fact, I believe it so firmly that I'm going out to the car to get my equipment for opening the tubes in the ear."

Neither Fred nor I believed that anything so simple could cause so much difficulty. The doctor returned with his instruments and went into Hentz's room. When he came out, he crossed over to us and said:

"Just as I thought. When the tubes were opened, the relief was instant. Without leaving dry land, Hentz had one of the most beautiful cases of seasickness I've ever seen!"

Mr. Sanders, from the Vocational Rehabilitation Department, stopped at the house to talk to Hentz. The Institute in New York wanted additional information on the patients who had been there, as a follow-up. The last question Mr. Sanders asked Hentz was:

"Hentz, do you have any suggestions to make to someone who might be hurt the way you were? Can you suggest anything that would enable them to come through as you have done—anxious to live a full life?"

I was curious as to what Hentz would reply, and his answer set my spirit to singing. He thought a while, and then said:

"Mr. Sanders, I haven't a suggestion to make. Not one. Whoever he may be, the poor fellow won't have a thing to do with the way he comes out of it. That depends entirely on the kind of family he happens to be born in."

Hentz was too modest to take any credit for his part of the fight, and he gave us too much, but it was good to hear. He didn't want to sound preachy and talk about faith —his and ours—but I knew that no family could do all that had to be done in a fight like this. You can encourage, smile, help, fight; but without a dependence on God for help, and faith that God will bring you through, you won't get through. During the day you may be able to make people believe you are doing fine, but in the silent darkness there will be the sobbing and despair I heard that night in the Miners' Ward. You can act gay during the day, but it takes more than acting to get through the nights when the audience is sleeping.

CHAPTER SIXTEEN

I had always thought that accepting financial assistance from State agencies would be extremely disagreeable to one's pride. It has not been so. The State Director, Mr. Paul Barrett, and Mr. A. P. Jarrell, who is in charge of the physical rehabilitation program, and Mr. Sanders, the counselor in Macon, have treated us with extreme courtesy and consideration. They act as though *they* were receiving the favor from us, instead of making it possible for Hentz to have expensive treatment.

For the past two years the State of Georgia has led the entire nation in the number of cases of rehabilitation, and money expended for such rehabilitation.

In a recent editorial in the *Atlanta Constitution*, Dr. Howard Rusk, Director of the Institute of Physical Medicine and Rehabilitation of the New York University–Bellevue Medical Center, said, "Georgia is the model for all states in the rehabilitation program."

In a letter to me, Dr. Rusk said: "I am glad to be able to tell you of the part that Georgia has played in rehabilitation. Georgia has long been a leader in rehabilitation among the other states; Georgia has not alone been a leader in the amount of money appropriated but in the spirit and carry-through of this most important program.

"I am sure that this stems from the State Director, Mr. Paul Barrett, and also his most able assistant, Mr. A. P. Jarrell. These two men, in particular, and the many vocational counselors who work under them have demonstrated the worthwhileness of a rehabilitation program, not alone from a humanitarian standpoint but also from the point of actual monetary return to the State, that the legislators and officers of the State now feel that this is not alone something that must be done, but is also a good investment. This has been proven time and time again just as it was by your son.

"To answer specifically to some of your questions, Georgia has always sent more patients to the Institute than any other State. I believe that Georgia, within the last few years, has appropriated more money than any other State in the Union, with California running a close second.

"I cannot emphasize enough that while the monies available are most important, it is still the deep understanding, the spiritual belief, and the hard-working team approach that are present in the Georgia State Vocational Rehabilitation program that make it outstanding.

"I hope this will answer your inquiry—actually, one could write a book on the activities of the Georgia program—and some day someone should do this."

Leadership is not accidental. There has to be a dream first —and Mr. Barrett and Mr. Jarrell had one. They believed that if sufficient money were appropriated to rehabilitate handicapped persons it would be good business for the State —apart from the good done to the ones who needed the rehabilitation. They have seen that dream worked out to their own satisfaction, and to the satisfaction of the governing powers of the State of Georgia.

In Perry there is a quality that I have never been able to define for myself accurately. Everyone who lives here a while knows it is here. If I had to use one word to describe what it is, the word would be "togetherness." In cities I suppose it is impossible to feel it; and I am conscious of its absence whenever I am in a large city. I don't think about it every moment that I am in Perry because I have come to accept it. But let trouble come, and the quality is there like a mother suddenly appearing in a darkened room to still her child. You give in to it; you lean on it; you know it won't fail you—and you thank God for it! Without it, I think we would have failed at some time during these difficult years.

This thing that is in Perry makes all of us know that there is a common tie that isn't necessarily social or spiritual. I am sure that not many people could name it but we all know of its existence. People in great cities are like the stars in the heavens, separated by the unknown spaces between them. Maybe some of them are tied together in groups, like the stars in the Big Dipper, but people in Perry are more like the freckles on a little boy's face. The spaces between the freckles are familiar and dear; what separates us is known and loved.

There is clannishness in Middle Georgia and in Perry, but it is giving way now, with economic changes. This clannishness accounts for part of the goodness of the people to us, but it does not account for all of it. There are other people who have been eager to help Hentz, and us, who were not prompted by devotion to clan. They hadn't married and intermarried among the descendants of the early settlers;

they were not even distant cousins of Fred and Hentz. Some of them have been here fifty years, some thirty years, and some came during the last World War. There are many in this last group, because Perry is now four times the size it was when I came here from Miami with Fred in 1930.

In an essay, "Still Rebels, Still Yankees," Donald Davidson explains the regionalistic nature of the people of our section. He says the good soil and the seasons that make almost anything grow account for the generous natures of the people in Middle Georgia. I had rather not think that rich land and agreeable seasons make people generous—I'd rather believe it was something spiritual. But it stands to reason that God didn't just dump this many good people in one spot.

Almost all of our neighbors own and operate large farms, and they share with friends who don't farm. Everyone who knows me knows of my passion for watermelon. One morning I looked out my front door and on the lawn was a truckload of *watermelons!* Pete Davis, our next-door neighbor, had sent them. When peaches are ripe, the peach growers divide the harvest; when friends catch fish in their lakes they share them; when figs are ripe neighbors send figs; and others share when they have peas, squash, okra, eggplant, pears, cantaloupe, and scuppernongs. Life is very good in Perry.

People in Perry do things with a flair, with a special touch. They do things just a little nicer, a little prettier, and with a little more taste than is required. They are not sleepy and backward. It is an astonishing place in many respects, and visitors are always impressed with our high standard of living.

When strangers ride through Perry, they know it is entered yearly in the Better Home Town Contests sponsored by the

Georgia Power Company. There are evidences of the pride, that is more than civic pride, everywhere. They see it when they pass the well kept homes; they sense it when they see the beautiful old churches and the new schools; they experience it when they stop to eat at the local hotel where tourists were being delighted by the tastefully prepared and perfectly served food long before Mr. Duncan Hines came on the scene with his stamp of approval.

Perry has changed since I came here as a bride—changed externally, I mean. Growth always changes the things we can see. In those days we didn't have much of anything except great quantities of leisure. As I think back on those times it seems that we did nothing but ride all morning, eat dinner—it is still at noontime here—then ride or go swimming or to a show until time for supper.

The endless leisure is gone. It is replaced by new homes well stocked with washing machines and babies. We no longer experience shock when we see a lovely young thing hanging clothes on a line in the back yard. Most people still have one servant, but with more children there is much that one servant cannot do.

If there is more work and less time to ride, there is also more money for trips and automobiles and good furniture. Golf has replaced the ladies' baseball team of old.

There is still plenty of time for people to be good neighbors, however. They have time to be with you when you're hurt and afraid. Routine duties can wait.

While I was away from home those many long months while Hentz was in the Macon Hospital, my friends and neighbors carried on things at home for me. I didn't come home until very late at night, and one neighbor took care of my mother for me. Because Mamma does not see well, and was afraid to stay alone until I came home, my friend took her to her home for supper and to spend the night.

We had a yard man who was supposed to come once a week and mow the grass, but sometimes he failed to show up. People would send their own yard men, or come themselves to do the mowing.

One of my neighbors watered our plants for an entire summer. Fred and I have a nice collection of camellias, but they would not have had a chance without water. Unless you've held a hose and fought gnats and bugs during August in Georgia, you can't appreciate this contribution. We didn't lose one of our prized plants. That was love!

Fred was in Perry during the day, and he always had more invitations to meals than he could possibly accept. The man and woman who own the Perry Hotel asked him to have his dinner as their guest every day, and he did accept their hospitality many times. He usually had his evening meal with his mother because he and his sisters rushed to the hospital as soon as they finished eating. This hospitality continued from the very first, and it went on while Hentz and I stayed in New York.

One friend with an engineering turn of mind designed an addition to the Foster bed that permitted Hentz to be turned at a forty-five-degree angle. In this way his face was spared the ordeal of being on the hard canvas, and at the same time the pressure on his back was relieved. Later, when Hentz came home from the Rehabilitation Center, the same man fixed the new hospital bed we had bought.

A contractor from another town constructed a concrete ramp at our back door and refused to accept pay for it.

When Hentz was in the hospital in Macon, a barber from Perry drove there whenever Hentz needed a haircut.

The telephone operators did so much to help too. When I would call Fred from New York they would keep trying our friends' homes until they located him. They would say, "Mrs. Houser, I'll try Mr. Beckham's house. Mr. Houser called his mother from there a little while ago."

Two young men from Brooklyn, New York, who hold the concession at the lake where Hentz was hurt, asked me if they could set one day aside and call it "Hentz Houser Day." It was a wonderful occasion. There were committees to see about every detail, and everyone in Perry was on some sort of committee. Every lady in the countryside baked a cake that was either sold or won at Bingo. Barbecue dinners were served, and there were contests and competition games. I couldn't go. I made myself believe that I didn't want to leave Hentz, but I knew that I didn't want to see the board and the water where Hentz had made his unfortunate dive. However, Fred, his sisters, and my mother attended, so the family was well represented. Between two and three thousand dollars was raised that day. It was given to Fred to use for Hentz.

Friends brought cold watermelons to the hospital and gallon freezers of homemade peach ice cream so that we could have a party on the screened porch.

Two or three of the drawers in Hentz's dresser served as our cupboard. Everyone in the hospital knew he could find the finest delicacies in those drawers. Though the nurses complained because there was no room for linens, they raided the cupboard too.

I suppose that every man and woman in Perry went to Fred and offered him money. Fred told me one day—and he said he was not exaggerating—that if it were necessary he could raise over half a million dollars before sundown. When friends beg you to use their money, you know their concern is genuine. We always knew that Hentz would not suffer because of a lack of funds.

Many other things were done for us too. One woman stayed in Fred's office for him during his lunch hour when his help was away for ten days. Fred's cousin, Francis Nunn, who owns a large warehouse, left his business during grain season, which was the busiest time of the year for him, to stay at the hospital. He stood by Hentz's bed for ten days moving Hentz's arms. Hentz wanted them moved constantly, and it was a tiring job. He stayed on one side of the bed and Ruth Rogers stayed on the other side. She had made her plane reservations for an exciting vacation when Hentz was hurt, but she canceled them. They are the ones who stayed in the room with Fred and me on the day we call Black Thursday.

Our neighbor, Pete, whom we love like a brother, called the insurance offices in Atlanta and instructed them to notify him if Fred forgot to send them checks. He said he would take care of everything. He didn't have to do so, because Fred returned to his office in time; but our neighbor wanted to spare Fred any embarrassment or inconvenience.

The president of the local bank assured Fred that he need never worry about a loan—it was always given without a question.

Our friend who owns the local funeral home—the one with the Cadillac ambulances—made many trips with Hentz. He usually did the driving himself rather than ask an employee, making trips to Macon, trips to Atlanta and back, and trips to planes. When we asked for a bill he sent one, but it had no amount on it. Written across the paper was: *Paid in full by the finest boy I know.*

When Christmas came a friend had a very handsome

wreath made for our front door. She knew that I would have had one if I'd been home.

The man who manages the local motion-picture theater told Hentz that he wanted him to be a lifetime guest of the theater.

When Hentz began his law course by correspondence, Perry lawyers offered to spend as much time with him as he thought he needed.

Two of the doctors in our town have convinced us that it gives them pleasure to come at any hour if we need them for Hentz. Dr. Hendrick and Mildred are always doing wonderful things for Hentz. Dr. Weems, a younger man who has been in Perry only a few years, and who has been unselfish in his eagerness to help us, gave Hentz a wire recorder so that he can record his lessons in the law course, and so that Betty or I can type them. They are not just doctors to us: they are very close friends. They have never let us pay them a cent. Dr. Felix Smith, the veterinarian, has taken care of the dogs during the years since Hentz's accident. They have had surgery and expensive care at no cost to us. He, too, says that we can't deprive him of the pleasure he derives from doing this for Hentz.

It is impossible to name *all* that has been done for us, because there is not one phase of our lives that has not been made easier and lovelier by the thoughtfulness of such people. We don't deserve it, but we accept these kindnesses with sincere gratitude.

Many people in New York have asked me: "What kind of boy is your son? What's he like?"

I would answer: "Why, what do you mean? He's just a boy." Then they would say, "He gets so much mail, and so many packages, we thought he must be some kind of celebrity."

And then I would tell them about Perry.

But I don't suppose I could really tell them—no more than I can tell you. How do you tell somebody what goodness is? Or love? Or compassion? The dictionary says they are excellence, or virtue, or a feeling of strong personal attachment, or sorrow or pity. But these are just words, and none of them—or any others—is capable of describing the help we've had. I've tried to name the *things* that were done, but there has been much more. Long after the memory of the gifts has blurred, we shall retain the knowledge that there are many hands ready to steady us if we feel afraid. This consciousness, together with the assurance of God's nearness, will keep us strong.

CHAPTER SEVENTEEN

"For God hath not given us the spirit of fear; but of power, and of love, and of a sound mind."—II Timothy, 1:7.

This morning, as I looked out my upstairs bedroom window, I saw two mockingbirds facing each other on the back lawn. They took a few graceful steps to the right, then to the left, and backward and forward. At first I thought they were sparring for a fight, but as I watched I delightedly realized that they were dancing with the precision of trained performers. How could they anticipate what their partner would do, and move precisely as he moved? Did they hear a sound range that I couldn't hear? Perhaps they did.

I turned from the window when the birds tired and flew away, and it seemed that I too heard music. With the music came a realization that shocked me. Why hadn't it come earlier? I felt a quiet kind of gladness and thankfulness. Something terrifying was gone, and was replaced by music and dancing birds, and a new happiness. For such a long time there had been an emptiness that held only the terrible hurt. It had been like an immense desert whose vastness and desolation were relieved by one lone cactus tree. But this day I knew that the emptiness was being filled again—perhaps the process had been going on for a long time, and it took the dancing mockingbirds to make it real.

As time passed we knew a happiness that we hadn't dared dream about—but with the happiness came repeated anxieties. Hentz's physical condition was worse, but in spite of that fact we experienced a kind of satisfying joy that we'd never known before. No longer do I torture myself wondering when God will let Hentz walk again. Now I know that happiness and walking are in no way associated. There is no connection between using your hands and finding contentment. Those things help, but there are paths to real contentment that can be traveled in a wheel chair. Sometimes the way may be rugged, but around almost every corner there are delights.

A line from an old Scottish ballad says appropriately how the years since Hentz was hurt have been: "I will lay me down and bleed a while, then rise and fight again." There were times when we had to lie down and bleed and lick our wounds. Some of those times I had wondered if I *could* rise and fight again—yet knowing all the while that I would. It is like complete physical exhaustion: you don't think you will ever be rested enough to get up and plod on. But God lets you sleep, and the agony and the aching and the weariness are gone with the night, and you awaken forgetful of the inertia and the lack of enthusiasm.

I could think of Hentz as being unable to walk or use his hands without feeling as though I'd been struck, and cringing and fighting to push it out of my mind. I don't remember striving toward happiness for myself, but I've prayed for Hentz to find it. In that way the thing I wanted for him came to me too.

I found release and pleasure working in the yard, and watching the growing things and the swelling buds. In Job 12:8 there is a quotation I've always loved, and found to be right: "Speak to the earth, and it shall teach thee." Many of the answers I've sought have come to me while I was working outdoors. When I graft camellias I feel the thrill of one who creates. When I cut down an unsatisfactory, unattractive bush and graft it with a scion from a lovely plant, I *think* I know how God must feel when we refuse the gift that could make us beautiful and productive. It is good to know that in two years the unlovely plant will bear blooms of great beauty. It is good for me to know that I can contribute to such transformation.

One cold, sunny day last winter we bought several camellia plants, and I had to decide where to place them. I was faced with the problem of giving each plant the best possible place. In our yard there were few spots that were perfect, and those had to be occupied by the fragile plants —the ones whose blooms cannot bear the burn of winter's frosts; the ones whose foliage wilts in the summer sun. I considered the traits and the degree of sturdiness of the new plants, and tried very hard to find the place best suited to each one. Was the shade too dense here? Would this tree sap the strength here? Would the afternoon sun be on it too long here? Suddenly it occurred to me that perhaps God was faced with the same kind of situation. Perhaps He knew our strength better than we did, and He was glad when we didn't wither under our adversities.

As we search for understanding, sometimes we find strange new substitutes. When we find acceptance and contentment and an end of the fight against despair, we've found a greater aid to happiness than hard cold logic. It doesn't matter *why* Hentz was hurt. What matters is how he has met the challenge. I believe that seeing him prove himself a man in the face of disaster has given me more real satisfaction than anything he could have accomplished as a physically strong person. Of course, I would have been proud to know that he had made a good life for himself and successful at whatever it was he would have been. But it wouldn't have been like this. Only the person familiar with the problems of a quadriplegic can realize how easy it would have been to *quit*. No phase of Hentz's life is simple; every move, every change is involved.

Knowing the will power and effort it takes for every small task makes the extra tasks he assigns to himself more significant. This fall, Guy Hutcherson, our minister, asked Hentz to talk at three meetings during Youth Week at the church.

Hentz doesn't like to have the attendant accompany him every place he goes because it lessens his feeling of independence, so he asked that the talks be given outdoors, on the church grounds. Hentz could go to the church in his electric chair, but if he went inside he would have to use the other chair. The electric chair is too heavy to be lifted up steps.

Fred and I drove to the church, which is in the center of a block, surrounded by trees. There were floodlights in the oak trees. We parked in the shadow of a tree so that we could see Hentz, but he couldn't see us. Hentz was sitting under a big oak, and the light came down on his head. In a little while ninety-three young people filed out of the church, and sat in the rows of folding chairs in front of Hentz. The night was very still, and the young people made no sound.

Then, in that clear, strong voice, that held no suggestion of weakness, Hentz began to talk. Neither Fred nor I spoke. Perhaps Fred was thinking of the time he told the doctor in Atlanta, "Our son will be better—you wait and see." What if Hentz couldn't walk? Suppose he had lived only until this night? Wouldn't this one night be worth all the fighting?

When Hentz finished speaking the young people gathered around his chair, and I could see him smiling and turning his head from one group to another. After a while the young people began doing folk dances in and out of the trees, and Hentz stayed to watch them. This time the sadness was not so great as I watched him looking upon his friends running and laughing. This time I knew he'd found inner resources to replace physical participation in the activities of youth. There was a catch in my heart, and I suppose there always will be, but it was a little one now, and it used to be a big one.

Fred and I drove away from our shadow, and I said, "He did well, didn't he?" I sounded complacent and a little the way I used to sound when Hentz had taken part in something at school. I wondered why I tried to hide from Fred the things I really felt.

He must have been hiding as much from me when he replied, "Yes, he certainly did!" Perhaps we had kept our guard up so long we couldn't let it down, not even when we were alone, and obviously sharing the same emotions.

When Hentz came home he looked unhappy. "I just did terribly—in fact I was a flop. I was sitting in front of a large electric fan, and the breeze blowing in my mouth made it very difficult for me to talk."

"We heard you, Hentz, and we think your talk was splendid." But he was not convinced.

In a few minutes Guy came rushing into the house, breathless and excited. He paced around the room, from one side of Hentz's bed to the other. He said: "Hentz, your talk tonight was the most inspirational experience of my entire life. Every young person there came to me and expressed what it meant to them. Boy, you should feel proud!"

Oh, I was thankful that Guy had come to see Hentz. Hentz knew Guy wouldn't tell an untruth, even to make him feel better. Perhaps Hentz thought Fred and I were so prejudiced that we were not capable of having an honest opinion.

Hentz said, "But my tongue was so dry that I could hardly talk."

"But you did talk! There was nothing wrong with the way you talked. And what you said won't ever be forgotten. If you were having speech difficulties, none of us knew it."

A twinkle come back in Hentz's eyes.

The next night Fred and I were parked in the shadow of the oak to hear Hentz talk on God's Circumstantial Will.

The third night Fred had to attend a meeting inside the church, and I listened to Hentz with a neighbor and my sister's little boy, Bill Bolin, who was visiting us from Arizona. On this last night Hentz's subject was God's Ultimate Will. As I watched him talking to the ninety young people, and heard his final sentence, "In the end God's ultimate will will be done, just as surely as the mountain stream reaches the ocean," I knew he spoke the truth. Disasters, sickness, pain, paralysis—none of them can crush whatever it is that keeps Hentz's spirit glowing, and eager to live every minute well.

As he finished the talk, I thought of something he'd said

when he was a little boy of five. We were driving through Arizona, and in the distance we saw an especially beautiful mountain. It was high and jagged and painted many colors. It made you think that it hadn't been touched since God finished it. Hentz pointed to one particularly impressive spot on the mountain, and said: "See that place right there? Some day, when I'm grown, I'm going to have a church there." I thought that he meant that surely people could be closer to God in such a spot—or perhaps he didn't know what he meant, except that the beauty reminded him of God.

The boy under the trees didn't have his church on the beautiful mountain. He was sitting outside the church where his father, his grandfather, and his great- and great-great-grandfathers had worshiped God. He was outside the church because his fierce pride made him refuse to be assisted up the high steps that led inside. But I could feel satisfaction that God's ultimate will was being fulfilled.

Hentz had been feeling particularly well and jovial. Many times he called me, and I would ask, "What do you want, son?"

He would answer, "Please sit down, I want to talk to you."

"What do you want to talk about?"

"Just how wonderful everything is. Life *is* wonderful, isn't it?" he would ask eagerly.

"Oh yes, yes! Life is very wonderful." I answered, and the joy I felt was the thunderous kind.

"And everything is so beautiful, too. Don't you think so?" He cocked his head and looked at me out of the corner of his eyes.

"And you are a very remarkable fellow." I always say it lightly.

One morning, after he had started to town in his electric chair, he called to me. I opened the kitchen door, thinking he had forgotten something and wanted me to bring it to him. The pale pink crabapple was in full bloom, the dogwoods were blooming, the late camellias were blooming, and the azaleas were blazing. But more miraculous than any of those things, was the smile on Hentz's face. As I walked close to him, he said, "Everything is so wonderful. Life is so very good."

Now I asked, trying to sound casual: "Has something special happened? Your chair must be running better than usual."

"No, nothing special. But life's so good and everything's so fine, and I get so full of it sometimes that I have to tell someone."

I touched him on the head, and made my stock reply, "You are the most remarkable lad."

"Remarkable? You say that so often. You know how I feel about myself? I think of myself as a normal human being, with nothing unusual about me at all. Honestly, I just never think about my condition one way or another until it is mentioned."

I swallowed very hard, and managed to say, "You wonderful crazy idiot!"

That night Hentz asked Fred and me to take him to a drive-in movie. The intimacy seemed to make him want to talk. He talked to Fred about some business matters, and plans for the future of the business. After awhile Hentz said, "You know, I'm happier now than I've ever been. I am more contented than I was before I was hurt." Fred and I didn't speak; at least, I don't remember anything we said; but my heart began singing, and it hasn't stopped—except for very

short periods when it forgets its song. Hentz continued, "I
don't mean that I'm satisfied with the life of a quadriplegic—
I'm not. And I intend to recover, but until that time comes,
I'm not unhappy."

I have prayed every day for a miracle. This is not what I
had in mind when I prayed, because to me the miracle was
for Hentz to walk again.

But, truly, I've seen a miracle.

In late October, 1954, Guy Hutcherson asked Hentz to
speak at the evening service at the church. Hentz told me
about it, saying, "I refused." I couldn't understand, and asked
him why he refused. Hentz laughed, and answered, "Guy
wanted me to close a series of sermons he's been giving called
The Life God Planned for You. Now I can't imagine myself
closing *that* series of talks!" Guy asked Hentz to talk in
December, and when he learned that the twelfth was Hentz's
birthday the talk was scheduled for that date.

Making any kind of plans must be undertaken with pre-
caution, because so many times we have to abandon them
or change them. It looked as though this time would be
no exception. Two weeks before December 12th, Hentz was
rushed to the Macon Hospital. He'd had another serious
hemorrhage from his bladder. For several hours the doctors despaired for his life. Guy visited Hentz at the hospital,
and when he asked Hentz if he thought he would be able to
make the talk, Hentz said: "I want to do it more than anything I know of, Preacher, but I don't know. We might as
well be practical, so perhaps you'd better not count on it."

The next morning Guy called me to ask what I thought
about announcing the talk in the church bulletin. He told
me that Hentz had said he wanted very much to do it.

"If Hentz wants to do it, he will do it." I declared. "I know that. I think it would indicate little faith if we didn't announce it, don't you? Go ahead and put it in the bulletin, but perhaps you'd better say Hentz will talk, 'God willing.'" Both of us knew that Hentz would be out of the hospital and make the talk.

When Hentz came home he was weak and very thin, but determined to make the scheduled talk. I worried about his breathing, and asked: "Do you think you can hold out to talk for thirty minutes? It will have to be louder than a conversational tone."

"Don't you worry! I'll get through it," he cheerfully replied.

The twelfth came, and with it came the day that my son was legally a man. I wrote him a little note, and part of it said, "It is a good thing to know—on this day when chronologically you become a man—that you are *every bit* a man!" I tried to tell him that he had more than fulfilled every dream I'd had about him, and that the first time I looked at him I prayed for God to make him a man of courage, a man of daring, and God-fearing and kind. I told him that God had answered that prayer completely.

Tracy drove down from Atlanta to hear Hentz's talk. There were the rushing and commotion that always takes place when all of us are going anywhere.

Hentz said he positively would not be rolled out to the pulpit after the crowd gathered, and insisted on going early so that he would be in the pulpit, waiting when the first ones arrived.

When my mother, Tracy, Louise, Leonora, and my next-door neighbor reached the church, there were cars parked around the entire block. We stopped for a moment in the vestibule, and I saw that the church was nearly filled. The usher took us to the second pew from the front. Hentz watched us as we were being seated, and I winked at him. I wanted him to think I felt very lighthearted about this occasion.

But I didn't feel lighthearted, and I wished desperately that I hadn't gone. I wanted to leave, but I knew I couldn't get out of the church without facing all the people. They would know I was weak. I straightened my back, and raised my head—and winked at Hentz again.

The church was filled long before the time for Hentz to speak. The ushers and young boys went into the Sunday-school rooms for folding chairs. They placed them down the aisles until there was room for no more; then they placed them between the front pew and the pulpit. Hentz calmly watched the activity. I wondered if he minded the people being so close to him. I thought I would feel smothered and trapped. I had never seen a larger crowd in the church.

The minister was sitting in one of the high-backed chairs in the pulpit that Fred's family had given in memory of his grandfather. He leaned over to whisper something to Hentz. My throat constricted with vise-like tightness when an usher offered Hentz a book, and he made no effort to reach out for it. The usher held it out again, forgetful that Hentz couldn't take the book from him. I saw Hentz shake his head very slightly, and smile a little as he turned away. I see those things, and I don't think anyone else sees them.

After Guy sang a solo, Hentz began his talk. His voice was strong at the beginning, but would it be strong thirty minutes from now? I began to pray. A childhood Sunday-school teacher had told me that we should ask God our favor, then forget it because God didn't like meaningless repetition. But I hoped that God would understand, and not be annoyed by my repetition, because I prayed at the end of every sentence Hentz uttered: "Dear God, let his breath hold out. Not for my pride, but for his. Please, please, don't let him give out of breath."

I did not once look at my son after he began his talk. I wanted to very much, so that I could cherish the expression that I knew was on his face. Instead I studied a board behind the piano that announced the number of persons who attended Sunday school today; the number attending this time last year; the number attending the Sunday before; and the collection for those dates. Over and over again I read the white letters.

I heard Hentz saying, "God allows pain in the world, because if we couldn't experience pain, we would be insensitive to joy and inspiration." I remembered that he'd asked me if I thought anyone would think he had reference to himself.

Finally the talk was finished. The crowd of people pushed to the front of the church. I sat still and watched. The ones who couldn't get close to Hentz chose Fred and me as poor substitutes. Hentz was happy, and responding to the kind words of his listeners. There seemed to be an endless stream of people in the aisles pressing toward Hentz, who was still in the pulpit.

These were our friends and neighbors, who through the years had demonstrated their sincerity in countless ways. Their comforting words, their prayers, their gifts had strengthened us—we always knew that we were not alone. This night, more than ever before, I knew that they too were a part of the miracle. This service was a homecoming for all of us; an occasion for rejoicing and the giving of thanks.

After a very long time, Fred rolled Hentz out of the church where more people remained to speak to him. As I walked out of the lovely old church where we had had Hentz baptized when he was a baby, and where we had given him over to God's watchful care, I knew definitely that that care had been diligent.

I stood under one of the trees and watched, and waited. I remembered those other birthdays spent in hospitals. We couldn't have known then that Hentz's twenty-first birthday would be like this. My pride in Hentz was great, and my gratitude was deep.

I pressed my face against the rough bark of the old tree, and thought it would be good to cry. I pressed my face harder against the tree and whispered: "God, for everything I thank you. Thank you!"

EPILOGUE

You who have read this moving story have probably made up your minds that Hentz could not live for long.

While this book was being readied for press, further surgery on Hentz was essential, but it did not save his life. Hentz died on August 7, 1955. As you read this you are probably wondering about his mother's reaction on learning that finally the fight had been lost. We have her permission to give you a little information about those last days and to quote some things she said.

It was an open secret between Hentz and his mother that she was writing this book, but he never asked to read a word of it. Finally, just before the operation, Hentz listened to a tape recording of the whole book. When the play-back was finished he said, "Mother, it is the most beautiful thing I ever heard," and his mother on hearing this opinion said, "No future sorrow could make me forget the glory of that moment. Hentz had taught me so much that when he died, I didn't even feel like crying. I felt that I was in the midst of something so much bigger than death, and that death was the loser. I even said, 'Thank you, God, for everything.'" She hopes that his story will have meaning for many people, and that his influence on others will not cease with his death.